T0354179

SEMIOTEXT(E) INTERVENTION SERIES

© Tiqqun, 2020

Published by Semiotext(e)
PO BOX 629, South Pasadena, CA 91031
www.semiotexte.com

Design: Hedi El Kholti

ISBN: 978-1-63590-092-7
Distributed by the MIT Press, Cambridge, Mass.,
and London, England
Printed in the United States of America

10 9 8 7 6 5 4 3 2

Tiqqun

The Cybernetic

Hypothesis

Translated by Robert Hurley

semiotext(e)
intervention
series □ 28

"We can dream of a time when—for good or ill, who knows?—the governing machine would rectify the obvious inadequacy of the leaders and the customary methods of the political system."
— Père Dominique Dubarle, *Le Monde*, December 28, 1948

"There is a striking contrast between the conceptual refinement and rigor that characterize scientific and technical procedures and the summary, imprecise style that characterizes political operations [...] One can't help but wonder if this might be an irremediable situation, marking the definitive limits of rationality, or whether one can hope that one day this impotence can be overcome and collective life will be completely rationalized at last."
— A cybernetician encyclopedist in the 1970s

HYPOTHESES ON THE HYPOTHESIS

Published for the first time in French in September of 2001, in the second issue of *Tiqqun*, "The Cybernetic Hypothesis" is not a *critical* text dealing with computers and cell phones, the internet and the web, social networks and GAFAM, digital work and the economy of platforms, big data and the power of algorithms, the capitalism of surveillance and the new digital economy, nor with immaterial workers and the postindustrial society, artificial intelligence and biotechnologies, facial recognition and deep learning, robots and transhumanism, etc. If it speaks directly or indirectly to all of these phenomena, and some others, if it anticipates certain questions that they raise today and will continue to raise tomorrow, with their still unpredictable developments, this is because it tries to grasp what they have in common *at its root*, in addition to the fact of peopling, shaping, and defining for a half-century the world in which we live and our everyday experience of it.

For at the origin of these new objects, there is in fact just a simple "hypothesis," but one very broad in scope, a general metaphysical conjecture concerning both social beings and natural beings (thus putting an end to one of the great divisions structuring Western thought) whose consequences have been deployed over a few decades in a multitude of domains of activity to the extent of redefining, profoundly and conjointly, the scientific and technical spheres, the mode of production, the regimes of subjectification and social relations, and, when all is said and done, the entire historical formation. In its most compact form, this is the hypothesis of "The Cybernetic Hypothesis." The near-disappearance, at the end of the 1970s, of the very term "cybernetic" in favor of other terms (systemic, cognitive, *informatique*, digital, *numérique*) deemed equivalent or close and seeking to describe, though always partially, the shifts of the current period, is one of the intriguing and paradoxical symptoms of the successful penetration of the cybernetic vision of the world. "It had to die in order to reign," as a friend aptly put it.

The originality of the text that follows derives from a "discovery" obscured by the numerous writings published on the subject of cybernetics even in the years that followed its publication : the cybernetic hypothesis would never have acquired its *practical hegemony* and its ability to reshape the world without having encountered in its course the history of capitalism and its two main protagonists, the States and the corporations.

Explicitly formed in the United States during World War II, the cybernetic project extracted itself from the scientific and technical discourses and practices and from the military universe in which it was born to metamorphose into a new general rationality of government of the public and the private only thanks to another political crisis, one that affected a vast part of the planet during the "years of 1968." The cybernetic *episteme* thus offers a *political* solution, as opposed to a purely technical one, to the becoming-ungovernable of the world's labor forces and populations. The seemingly inoffensive category of "digital culture," sometimes used to unify the phenomena resulting from the deployment of the cybernetic hypothesis, is not only partial, it is deceptive, pernicious even, since it ignores this political dimension and the active role of the cyberneticians and their allies in the social war.

This text suggests on the contrary that what today is called neoliberalism is best understood as *cybernetic capitalism*. A number of traits characteristic of neoliberal political and economic formations, widely observed and described for twenty years, beginning with the place now held therein by financial capital and its anticipations, would be fully grasped in fact, or enriched, on the basis of this more accurate designation. And the history of cybernetic approaches and techniques [*savoirs*], which have developed considerably since 2001, after all, would benefit from including within its scope of inquiry, management, finance, and political science, in addition to the economy and the sciences of the living.

In our text here, we can say that spotting the cybernetic hypothesis even in apparently disparate domains was the means of restoring, beyond their dispersal, their polymorphism, and their fragmentation, the hidden unity of a collection of distant, heterogeneous facts that nonetheless compose a single tableau. It was all the more necessary to outline this subterranean base—even in the form of a sketch—given that this hypothesis was itself the explicit product of a fantasy of totalization in individuals afflicted by a melancholy of totality caused by the Western epistemological crisis of the turn of the 19th century and the subsequent European civil war—the pages that follow emphasize this repeatedly. The cybernetic totalization is not, however, simply "antitotalitarian." It is an integral alternative to the total commodification and the state totalization whose major economic or political crises it aims above all to mitigate. What had been a fatal weakness was to change definitively into an indispensable asset. With the tendential autonomization of the cybernetic instruments and machines vis-à-vis markets, firms, and states, information technology aspires to form the sole basis of both value and power. Quantification and evaluation become both essential and ordinary operations of collective life. The digitalization of organizations, then that of domestic spaces, currently in the process of completion, are seen as one of the principal vectors of this great transformation. What used to be called "private," intimate life, subjectivity, the body and all of living existence are now invested and colonized by capitalistic and state powers to a degree that would have appeared unthinkable and intolerable to previous generations.

For the obsession with risk is the flip side of this accumulation of data, the privileged site where the military origin of cybernetics is revealed. Which explains the current hypertrophy of security operations and functions—prediction, surveillance, repression, incarceration, which are tightening their often hidden, discreet, invisible hold, at the same time that the apparatuses inspired by the hypothesis are expanding. Cybernetic government is an *ultrapolice*, a contemporary and planetary mode, imperial in this sense, of conspiracy with strategic implications for what another text of *Tiqqun 2*, complementary with it in many respects, calls the "civil war." The analysis that follows announced the extent to which the communications, the closenesses, the linkages, the emancipations that the technological developments of the past decades seem to have enabled have actually come at the price of a tentacular control, to the point that one has been able to speak rightly of "control societies" to describe the effect of the new art of governing that has been installed in several countries of the world counting from the 1970s. While avoiding a collapse, all the institutions, starting with law, are shaken by the innovation. The coordinates of exploitation, alienation, and domination are also put at risk as are that of their critique and the politics that results from it. The text doesn't open by chance with the historical motif of the cybernetic hypothesis overshadowing the "liberal hypothesis" stemming from the bourgeois revolutions. All the supports of political liberalism are or will be shaken, one after the other, as we have seen since 2001. Humanist culture and the metaphysics of the subject are no longer of any philosophical or ethical help against the machinery they are facing. Even when they are libertarian, those in command of the operations couldn't care less about "the rights of man and of the citizen."

The effects of cybernetic apparatuses multiplying communications and controls on the exercise of classic politics can only be ambiguous. All the organs of production and representation of interests, starting with the unions, the parties, the media, are contested in favor of scattered and fragmentary structures that are more flexible, less bureaucratic or vertical, and more ephemeral. By giving a public voice to those who didn't have one or by *imposing* participation or deliberation on the many, the cybernetic mutation of politics validates collectives, minorities and the margins. But in addition to a better intelligence and a more precise knowledge of the population, this democratic *redistribution of speech* is paired with an extraordinary individualization and rationalization of propaganda. The cybernetized public space is the consummation of postmodernism: discourse is shattered, truth is indiscernable, and relativism is the new norm. So the celebration of horizontality and the fervent activism on the new media are not in any way contradictory with the more and more blatant emergence—the U.S. launched this trend—of *cybernetic leaders* who owe their conquest of power to the new communication technologies and are using them to construct their charismatic authority. The whole panoply of authoritarian regimes, with their free elections, was thus given a new impetus, readied for a new set of applications which the Chinese rulers have taken up and are showing the way to all the others.

The cybernetic horizon of a self-regulation of living social beings proceeding without noise or friction is an ideal that cannot be fully realized, however. The cybernetic evolution of societies does not proceed without resistances nor without breakaways. But under cybernetic duress, the forms of critical theory tend to find themselves neutralized as a simple moment of a feedback loop. "The Cybernetic Hypothesis" devotes several passages to this problem from which it attempts to draw conclusions for its own writing. The political devaluation of veridiction and the surveillance of revolutionary authors which cybernetic apparatuses lead to require a language that is deliberately allusive and allegorical at first. This should be kept in mind when reading the variations that follow concerning a politics of invisibility, jamming, pulsation, panic, or guerilla warfare. Beyond a new language for politics, a *new strategy* of historical overthrow is hazarded in these passages. And it's to this same enunciative experiment that one owes no doubt the stupefaction felt by certain readers discovering that even before the events of September 2011, reference had been made by the authors of "The Cybernetic Hypothesis" to the strategic theory of the Arab revolt elaborated by T.E. Lawrence, which appeared to anticipate the actions of the Al-Qaeda combatants and the response that was given them.

Tiqqun's meditations on the modes of dissipation of cybernetic capitalism converge in the recognition of a battle in progress, nay a war, to break the "monopoly on autonomy" through the multiplication and spread of "zones of offensive opacity" involving all territories and in every practical sphere. In opposition to the notion of "temporary autonomous zones" (TAZ), then in vogue within North American and global anarchism, the idea is not reducible, either, to "liberated communes" or to "zones to be defended" (or "zones of definitive autonomy"). But the world of "hacking" is certainly made up of these "zones of offensive opacity" that border on armies of more or less mercenary cyberwarriors in the service of the states. Although these suggestions were published nearly twenty years ago, a major effort still needs to be made in order to give an extensive practical and theoretical consistency to the political horizon of these zones of offensive opacity.

Sooner or later, the question of "the intensification of their relations," as the authors write, will finally be formulated. Will such a perspective be able to free itself from the figure of the network as it has emanated from the cybernetic way of thinking? Hasn't the latter managed to neutralize the whole charge of opacity which the notion contained coming out of the Second World War? Hasn't the reticular image become the privileged way to understand a multiplicity of processes of integration of parts into a whole and of articulation of the small and the large? And what *détournement* of the use of cybernetic apparatuses would cause them to serve the revolutionary perspective instead of preventing its florescence? The cybernetic spirit, that of the second cybernetics in particular, has not always been a stranger to revolt nor even to autonomy, and vice versa. Whatever one may think of those forgotten connections, those ephemeral experimentations, those failed or all-too successful encounters, let us simply recall that the cybernetic environments do not develop without fractures or fractions and that every governmentality is reversible. Nothing prohibits *in theory* the invention of seditious uses of the digital technologies. Although the authors of "The Cybernetic Hypothesis" are never affirmative to this degree, they are careful to keep their distance from the debates of their era opposing technophiles and technophobes. The fact is that a whole part of the social critique of capitalism has taken refuge for several decades in a critique of technics. If "The Cybernetic Hypothesis" enables one to understand the reasons for this retreat, it does not endorse the move.

Determining what autonomy will be capable of dynamiting the autonomy of cybernetics is therefore one of the problems bequeathed by this text. Other intuitions it contains will need to be extended, tested, actualized. That is why its publication in English in the U.S. is welcome at this time. One can imagine that a majority of its readers will be found among the digital natives. Reading its pages, which may look dated to them in places, they will take the measure of what has made them without their doing anything. And, like us, the measure of what remains for them to do.

— Paris, November 2019

I

"There is probably no area of thought or of man's material activity in which one can say that cybernetics will not, sooner or later, have a role to play."
— Georges Boulanger, *Le dossier de la cybernétique dans le monde d'aujourd'hui*, 1968

"The great concentrator wants stable circuits, even cycles, predictable repetitions, untroubled accountability. It wants to eliminate every partial drive, it wants to immobilize the body. Such is the anxiety of the emperor of whom Borges speaks, who demanded a map of the entire empire so exact that it had to cover the entire territory in every aspect and therefore duplicate its scale exactly, to such an extent that the monarch's subjects spent so much time and used up so much energy in putting the finishing touches to it and maintaining it that the empire 'itself' fell more and more into ruin as its cartographic blueprint became more and more perfect—such is the madness of the great central Zero, its desire to bring a body, which can only 'be' if it is represented, to a standstill."
— Jean-François Lyotard, *Économie libidinale*, 1973

"WHAT THEY DESIRE IS AN ADVENTURE and to live that adventure with you. That's really the only thing one can say. They firmly believe that the future will be modern: different, exciting, difficult no doubt. Full of cyborgs and guileless entrepreneurs, market fevers and animal robots. *Which is already true in the present for those willing to see.* They think the future will be human, even feminine—and pluralist; and would like everyone to experience it, to take part in it. They're the enlightened ones we had lost, the foot soldiers of progress, the inhabitants of the 21st century. They're fighting ignorance, injustice, poverty, suffering of every kind. You'll find them where things are stirring, where something is happening. They don't intend to miss anything. They're humble and courageous, serving an interest that goes beyond them, guided by a higher principle. They know how to frame problems but also find solutions. They'll lead us across the most perilous frontiers, extend a hand from the shores of the future. They are History in motion, at least what's left of it, because the roughest stretch is behind us. They are saints and prophets, true socialists. They understood a long time ago that May 1968 was not a revolution. *The real revolution* is what they're doing. It's now just a question of organization and transparency, of intelligence and cooperation. An immense program! And..." Wait. Excuse me, but WHAT ARE YOU SAYING? What program? The worst nightmares, you know, are often the metamorphoses of a fable, the kind of story THEY would tell us children to put us to sleep and round out our moral education. The new conquerors, whom we shall call cyberneticians here, don't form an organized party—which has made the task easier—but a diffuse constellation of agents, motivated, possessed, blinded by the same fable. They are the killers of time, the crusaders of the Same, the lovers of fatality. They're the believers in order, the lovers of reason, the *people of transitions.* The Grand Narratives may well be dead as the postmodern vulgate reminds over and over again, but domination is still constituted by master fictions. This was the case with that *Fable of the Bees* that Bernard de Mandeville published in the first years of the 18th century and that helped so much to establish political economy and justify the advances of capitalism. There prosperity and the social and political order no longer depended on the Catholic virtues of sacrifice but on each individual's pursuit of their own interest. In that story the "private vices" were declared to be guarantors of the "common good." Thus, contrary to the religious spirit of his time, Mandeville, "the Man-Devil," as he was called back then, founded the *liberal hypothesis* that would later inspire Adam Smith. Although it is regularly reactivated in the renovated forms of liberalism, that particular fable is now outmoded. For critical minds, *liberalism is no longer the thing to critique.* Another model has taken its place, the one that hides behind the names of Internet, new information and communication technologies, "New Economy," or genetic engineering. Liberalism is now just a residual justification, the alibi for the daily crime committed by cybernetics.

Rationalist critiques of the "economic faith" or of "the neo-technological utopia," anthropological critiques of utilitarianism in the social sciences and the hegemony of commodity exchange, Marxist critiques of "cognitive capitalism" as opposed to the "communism of the multitudes," political critiques of a communication utopia that allows the worst fantasies of exclusion to resurface, critiques of critiques of "the new spirit of capitalism" or critiques of the "penal state" and of the surveillance that conceals itself behind neoliberalism— the critical minds seem reluctant to consider the emergence of *cybernetics as a new technology of government* that groups together and associates discipline and biopolitics, police and advertising, its precursors which are not effective enough nowadays in the exercise of domination. This is to say that cybernetics is not, as it tends to be understood, just the separate sphere of production of information and communication, a virtual space that would be superimposed on the real world. It has become clear that cybernetics is rather *an autonomous world of apparatuses merged with the capitalist project insofar as the latter is a political project*, a gigantic "abstract machine" made up of binary machines deployed by Empire, a new form of political sovereignty, and, it must be said, *an abstract machine that has turned into a global war machine*. Deleuze and Guattari correlate this development to a new form of appropriation of war machines by nation-states: "It was only after the Second World War that automatization, and then the automation of the war machine, produced their true effect. Taking into account the new antagonisms that traversed it, the war machine no longer had war as its exclusive object, but took charge of peace and politics, with world order as the goal, in short. It is here that the inversion of Clausewitz's formula appears: politics becomes the continuation of war; *it is peace that liberates technically the unlimited material process of total war.* War ceases to be the materialization of *the war machine; the war machine itself becomes materialized warfare.*" For this reason, the cybernetic hypothesis is not something to be criticized either. It is to be combated and defeated, which is a question of time.

The *cybernetic hypothesis* is thus a political hypothesis, a new fable that, beginning with the Second World War, has definitively supplanted the liberal hypothesis. Unlike the latter, it would have us think of biological, physical, and social behaviors as being integrally programmed and reprogrammable. More exactly, it imagines every behavior as being "piloted" in the last instance by the survival imperative of a "system" which makes it possible and to which it must contribute. It's a theory of equilibrium originating in a context of crisis. Whereas 1914 exacted its penalties for the decomposition of the anthropological conditions supporting the liberal hypothesis—the emergence of Bloom, the breakdown, manifested in flesh and blood in the trenches, of the idea of the individual and of any metaphysics of the subject—and 1917 served as its historical contestation with the Bolshevik "revolution," 1940 marks the extinction of the idea of society, enfeebled as it obviously was by the totalitarian self-destruction. As limit experiences of political modernity, Bloom and totalitarianism have been the most solid refutations of the liberal hypothesis. Moreover, what Foucault will playfully call "the death of Man" is nothing more that the ravage caused by these two skepticisms, the first directed at the individual, the second at society, and provoked by the Thirty Years War that beset Europe and the world during the first half of the last century. The problem posed by the *Zeitgeist* of those years is again to "defend society" against the forces that lead to its decomposition, to restore the social totality despite a general crisis of presence that afflicts each of its atoms. So the cybernetic hypothesis answers, in the natural sciences and social sciences alike, to a desire for order and certainty. The most effective organization of a cluster of reactions motivated by an active desire for totality, and not only by a nostalgia for the latter as in the different variants of Romanticism, the cybernetic hypothesis has a kinship with the totalitarian ideologies and all the holisms—be they mystical, solidarist as in Durkheim, functionalist, or indeed Marxist. It is their next generation, picking up where they leave off.

As an ethical position, the cybernetic hypothesis is complementary, though strictly contrary, to the humanist pathos that rekindles its flame as early as the 1940s and is nothing but an attempt to proceed as if "Man" can be considered intact after Auschwitz, an attempt to reinstate the classic metaphysics of the subject in spite of totalitarianism. But whereas the cybernetic hypothesis includes the liberal hypothesis while superseding it, humanism only aims to extend the liberal hypothesis to more and more situations that are resistant to it: it's all the corporatist "bad faith" of a Sartre for example—to turn one of his lamest categories back against him. The constitutive ambiguity of modernity, superficially regarded either as a disciplinary process or a liberal process, as a realization of totalitarianism or liberalism's coming-of-age, is contained and suppressed in, with, and by the new governmentality that is emerging, inspired by the cybernetic hypothesis. The latter is nothing other than the *protocol for full-scale experimentation* of the Empire in formation. By producing devastating truth effects, its realization and its extension are already corroding all the institutions and social relations based on liberalism and are transforming the nature of capitalism as well as the chances of contesting it. The cybernetic gesture asserts itself by a negation of everything that escapes regulation, of all the lines of escape that save existence in the interstices of the norm and its apparatuses, of all the behavioral fluctuations that ultimately would not follow from natural laws. To the extent that it has managed to produce its own veridictions, the cybernetic hypothesis is now *the most substantial anti-humanism*, one that is determined to maintain the general order of things while priding itself on having gone beyond the human.

Like every discourse, the cybernetic hypothesis has been able to verify itself only by assimilating the beings or ideas that reinforce it, testing itself through their contact, bending the world to its laws in a continuous process of self-validation. It has become a set of apparatuses whose ambition is to take charge of the totality of existence and the existent. The greek *kubernèsis* means, in the literal sense, "the action of piloting a vessel," and in the figurative sense, "the action of ruling, of governing." In his course of 1981-1982, Foucault emphasizes the significance of this category of "piloting" in the Greek and Roman world while suggesting that it could very well have a more contemporary relevance: "I think the idea of piloting as an art, as a theoretical and practical technique necessary to existence, is an important idea which might be worth analyzing more closely, inasmuch as at least three types of techniques are usually associated with this model of piloting: first, medicine; second, political government; third, the direction and government of oneself. In Greek, Hellenistic, and Roman literature, these three activities (curing, leading others, and governing oneself) were regularly analyzed by reference to the image of piloting. And I think that this image of piloting picks out quite well a type of knowledge (*savoir*) and practices between which the Greeks and the Romans recognized a definite kinship and for which they sought to establish a *tekné* (an art, a reflected system of practices referring to general principles, notions, and concepts): The Prince, insofar as he must govern others, govern himself, and cure the ills of the city, of citizens and of himself; the person who governs himself as one governs a city, by curing his own ills; the doctor, who has to give his views not only on bodily ills but on the ills of the souls of individuals. In short, I think there is here a whole batch, a set of notions in the mind of the Greeks and Romans which, I think, fall within the province of a single type of knowledge (*savoir*), a single type of activity, and a single type of conjectural knowledge (*connaissance*). And I think we could follow the entire history of this metaphor practically up to the sixteenth century, at which point, precisely, the definition of a new art of governing centered around *raison d'État* will draw a radical distinction between government of oneself, medicine, and government of others, but not without this image of piloting remaining linked, as you know very well, to the activity that is called, precisely, the activity of government."

What Foucault's audience is said to *know very well*, and what he chooses not to explain, is that by the end of the 20th century, the image of piloting, that is, of management, has become the cardinal metaphor for describing not just politics but also every human activity. Cybernetics becomes the project of a rationalization without limits. In 1953, when he publishes *The Nerves of Government*, during the peak period of development of the cybernetic hypothesis in the natural sciences, Karl Deutsch, an American social sciences professor, takes seriously the political possibilities of cybernetics. He recommends abandoning the old nationalist conceptions of power that have too long constituted the essence of politics. Governing will be inventing a rational coordination of information flows and decisions that circulate in the social body. Three conditions, he says, will make this possible: installing a set of *sensors* to ensure that no information coming from the "subjects" is lost; *processing information* through correlation and association; and placing oneself in *proximity* to every living community. The cybernetic modernization of power and of the outmoded forms of social authority declares itself therefore as a visible production of Adam Smith's "invisible hand" which served up to then as the mystical keystone to liberal experimentation. The communication system would be the nervous system of societies, the source and destination of all power. *In this way the cybernetic hypothesis sets out the politics of the "end of politics," neither more nor less.* It represents both a paradigm and a technique of government.

Its study shows that the police apparatus is not just an organ of power but also a form of thought.

Cybernetics is the police thought of Empire, entirely driven, historically and metaphysically, by an *offensive conception of politics*. Today it is finishing the business of integrating the techniques of individuation—or separation—and totalization that had developed separately: normalization, "anatamo-politics," and regulation, "biopolitics" to put it like Foucault. I call *the policing of qualities* its techniques of separation. And, following Lukàcs, I call *the social production of society* its techniques of totalization. With cybernetics, production of singular subjectivities and production of collective totalities mesh together to replicate History in the form of a *false movement* of evolution. It creates the fantasy of a Same that always manages to integrate the Other: as a cybernetician explains it, "every real integration is based on a prior differentiation." In this regard, no one has been better than the "automaton," Abraham Moles, its most zealous French ideologue, at expressing that pure death drive which impels cybernetics: "It's conceivable that a society taken as a whole, a State, could be regulated in such a way that it is protected from all future accidents: such that in itself only eternity changes it. *This is the ideal of a stable society achieved through objectively controllable social mechanisms.*" Cybernetics is warfare directed against all that lives and all that lasts for a time. In studying the formation of the cybernetic hypothesis, what I offer here is *a genealogy of imperial government.* I then set it in contrast with other ways of warfare, which it effaces on a daily basis and by which it will end up being overthrown.

II

"*Synthetic life is certainly one possible product of our evolving techno-bureaucratic control, or the return of the entire planet to the inorganic level, another possible outcome—ironically enough—of the same revolution in control technology.*"
— James R. Beniger, *The Control Revolution,* 1986

Although the origins of the Internet apparatus are now well known, it may be useful to underscore their *political significance* again. The Internet is a *war machine* invented through analogy with the highway system—which was also conceived by the American military as a decentralized tool of internal mobilization. The American armed forces wanted a network that would preserve the command structure in the event of nuclear attack. The response consisted of an electronic network capable of automatically redirecting information even if nearly all the links were destroyed, thus allowing the surviving authorities to stay in communication with one another and to make decisions. With such an apparatus, military authority could be maintained against the worst of catastrophes. So the Internet is the result of a *nomadic transformation of military strategy*. With this sort of planning at its root, one may be skeptical of the alleged anti-authoritarian characteristics of the apparatus. Like the Internet, which it derives from, cybernetics is an *art of war* whose objective is to save the head of the social body in the case of catastrophe. What emerged historically and politically during the interwar period, and what the cybernetic hypothesis responded to, was the metaphysical problem of establishing order starting from disorder. The whole scientific edifice, in what it owed to the deterministic assumptions embodied in Newton's mechanistic physics, crumbled in the first half of the century. The sciences of this era must be imagined as territories torn between the neo-positivist restoration and the probability revolution, and then groping toward a historic compromise whereby laws could be redefined on the basis of chaos, and certainty on the basis of probability. Cybernetics passes through this movement— begun in Vienna at the turn of the century, then carried to England and the United States in the thirties and forties. It constructs a *Second Empire of Reason* from which the idea of the Subject, until then considered indispensable, is absent. As a body of knowledge, it brings together a set of heterogeneous discourses that all address the *practical problem of mastering uncertainty*. What they express fundamentally, in their various domains of application, is the desire for an order to be restored and, further, that it have the stability to endure.

The founding scene of cybernetics takes place among the scientists in a context of total war. It would be futile to look for some malicious reason or the traces of a conspiracy there: one finds simply a handful of ordinary men mobilized for America during the Second World War. Norbert Wiener, an American scientist of Russian origin, is charged with developing along with a few colleagues a *machine for predicting and monitoring* the positions of enemy aircraft for the purpose of destroying them. At the time, it was only possible to foresee with any certainty correlations between some of an airplane's positions and some of its behaviors. The design of the "Predictor," the forecasting machine demanded of Wiener, required a specific method for processing the plane's positions and for gauging the interactions of a weapon with its target. *The entire history of cybernetics is concerned with getting around this impossibility of determining at the same time the position and the behavior of a body.* Wiener's intuition consists in *translating the problem of uncertainty into a problem of information*, in a temporal series where certain data are already known, others not yet known... and in *considering the object and the subject of the knowledge as a whole*, a "system." The solution consists in constantly introducing into the interplay of the initial data *the observed gap* between the desired behavior and the actual behavior, so that they coincide when the gap is eliminated, like the operation of a thermostat. The discovery goes well beyond the boundaries of the experimental sciences:

controlling a system would depend finally on establishing a circulation of information called "feedback," or recursion. The significance of these findings for the natural and social sciences is explained in a work published in 1948 in Paris under the enigmatic title *Cybernetics*, which, for Wiener, designated the doctrine of "control and communication in the animal and the machine."

Thus cybernetics emerges with the harmless appearance of a mere theory of information, information without any precise origin, always-already there potentially in an environment of whatever situation. It claims that *control of a system can be obtained through an optimal degree of communication between its parts*. That objective requires first of all a continuous extortion of information, a process of separation of beings from their qualities, of production of differences. To put it in other terms, *the mastery of uncertainty proceeds by way of the representation and memory storage of the past*. On the one hand, the spectacular image, binary mathematical codification—the kind invented by Claude Shannon and presented in *A Mathematical Theory of Communication* the very same year that the cybernetic hypothesis was presented—and on the other, the invention of memory machines that don't alter the information, and the incredible effort that went into their miniaturization, which is the decisive strategic function of present-day nanotechnologies. These elements conspire to create the right conditions at the collective level. Formatted in this manner, the information must then return to the world of beings, binding them to each other, in the same way that the circulation of commodities guarantees their placing into equivalence. Feedback, the key to the regulation of the system, now demands a *communication* in the strict sense. Cybernetics is the project of recreating the world through the infinite looping together of these two moments: representation that separates, communication that binds, the first dealing death, the second mimicking life.

The cybernetic discourse begins by shelving as so many false problems the 19th century controversies pitting the mechanist views against the vitalist or organicist views of the world. It posits a functional analogy between living organisms and machines, assimilated under the notion of "system." Hence the cybernetic hypothesis justifies two types of scientific and social experimentations. The first aims at *making living beings into a mechanics*, at mastering, programming, determining humans and their life, society and its "future." It fuels the return of eugenics as well as the bionic fantasy. It seeks to place the end of History on a scientific footing: here initially one is on the terrain of control. The second aims at *imitating the living with machines*, first as individuals, and this leads to the development of robots and artificial intelligence; next as collectives and this involves the setting of information into circulation and the construction of networks. Here one is situated rather on the terrain of communication. Although socially made up of very diverse populations—biologists, doctors, computer specialists, neurologists, engineers, consultants, police officers, publicists, etc.—the two currents of cyberneticians are nonetheless united by the shared fantasy of the Universal Automaton, analogous with Hobbes' fantasy of the State in *Leviathan*, "artificial man (or animal)."

The unity of the cybernetic advances is owing to a method—that is, it has imposed itself as a *method of inscription* of the world, an experimental mania and a proliferating schematism at the same time. It corresponds to the explosion of applied mathematics resulting from the despair caused by the Austrian Kurt Gödel when he showed that any attempt at laying a logical foundation for mathematics and unifying the sciences thereby, was doomed to "incompleteness." With the help of Heisenberg, more than a century of positivist justification had just collapsed. It was Von Neumann who gave an extreme expression to this feeling that the underpinnings had been obliterated. He interpreted the logical crisis as a mark of the inescapable imperfection of every human creation. He wanted to establish, consequently, a logic that would finally manage to be coherent, a logic that could only come from the automaton. From being a pure mathematician he became the agent of a scientific mélange, a general mathematization that would make it possible to reconstruct from below, in practice, the lost unity of the sciences, of which cybernetics would be the most stable theoretical expression. Subsequently there has been no demonstration, no discourse, no book, no place that is unaffected by the universal language of the explanatory schema, by the *visual form of reasoning*. Cybernetics transports the process of shared rationalization to bureaucracy and to capitalism at the stage of *total modeling*. In the 1960s, Herbert Simon, the prophet of Artificial Intelligence, takes up Von Neumann's program in order to construct an *automaton of thinking*. This consists of a machine equipped with a program called *expert system* designed to be capable of *processing information* to solve the familiar problems of every domain of special expertise, and by association, the whole range of practical problems encountered by humanity! The *General Problem Solver* (GPS), created in 1972, is the model of that universal expertise which synthesizes all the others, the model of all models, the applied intellectualism par excellence, the practical realization of that favorite adage of little masters without mastery which says, "There are no problems, just solutions."

The cybernetic hypothesis progresses as theory and as technology indistinctly, the one always certifying the other. In 1943, Wiener meets John Von Neumann, tasked with constructing machines quick and powerful enough to do the calculations necessary to the development of the Manhattan Project on which 15,000 scientists and engineers plus 30,000 technicians and laborers will work under the direction of the physicist Robert Oppenheimer: the computer and the atomic bomb are born together. Thus, from the point of view of the contemporary imagination, the myth of "the utopia of communication" is complementary to that of the invention of the nuclear monster: it's always a matter of *finishing off our being-together* through excess of life or through excess of death, through earthly fusion or through cosmic suicide. Cybernetics presents itself as the appropriate response to the Great Fear of the destruction of the world and of the human species. Von Neumann is its double agent, the "inside outsider" if there ever was one. The analogy between the categories for describing his machines and living organisms and those of Wiener seals the alliance between cybernetics and information technology. It will take several years for molecular biology, at the origin of the decoding of DNA, to use information theory to explain man as an individual and as a species, thereby conferring an unequaled technical power on the experimental genetic manipulation of human beings.

The shift from the metaphor of the system towards that of the network in social discourse between the 1950s and the 1980s points to the other fundamental analogy constituting the cybernetic hypothesis. It also indicates a profound transformation of the latter. For if "system" was talked about, between cyberneticians, this was by comparison with the *nervous system*, and if today "network" is talked about in the cognitive sciences it's the *neural network* that THEY have in mind. Cybernetics is the assimilation of the entirety of existing phenomena to those of the brain. By *positing the head as the alpha and omega of the world*, cybernetics guaranteed it would always be at the vanguard of vanguards, the one behind which all the others were always running to keep up. At its beginning, in fact, it establishes an *identity between life, thought, and language*. This radical monism is based on an analogy between the notions of information and energy. Wiener introduces it by grafting onto his discourse that of thermodynamics. The operation

consists in comparing the effect of time on an energy system with the effect of time on an information system. A system, as system, is never pure and perfect: there is a deterioration of energy as it is exchanged just as there is a degradation of information as it circulates. This is what Clausius named *entropy*. Entropy, considered as a natural law, is the cybernetician's Hell. It explains the decomposition of the living, disequilibrium in the economy, the dissolution of the social bond, decadence… In a first, speculative, phase cybernetics thus claimed to be founding the shared terrain on the basis of which the unification of the natural sciences and the human sciences would be possible.

What will be called "second-order cybernetics" will be the superior project of an experimentation on human societies: an *anthropotechnics*. The cybernetician's mission is to combat the general entropy that threatens living beings, machines, societies, that is, to create the experimental conditions for a continuous revitalization, to constantly restore the integrity of the whole. "The important thing is not that man be present but that he exist as the living medium for the technical idea," observes the humanist commentator Raymond Ruyer. With the elaboration and development of cybernetics, the ideal of the experimental sciences, already at the origin of political economy *via* Newtonian physics, lends its support to capitalism once more. Subsequently "contemporary society" will come to be what THEY call the laboratory where the cybernetic hypothesis is tested out. Since the end of the 1960s, thanks to the techniques it has taught, *second-order cybernetics is no longer a laboratory hypothesis but a social experiment.* It aims to construct what Giorgio Cesarano describes as a stabilized animal society that "[for termites, ants, bees] has automatic functioning as its natural presupposition, involving the negation of the individual: in this way the animal society as a whole (termite mound, anthill, or hive) presents itself as a plural individual, whose unity determines, and is determined by the division of roles and functions—in the framework of an 'organic composition' in which it is hard not to see the biological model of the teleology of Capital."

III

"No prophecy is necessary to recognize that the sciences now establishing themselves will soon be determined and piloted by the new fundamental science which is called cybernetics. This science corresponds to the determination of man as an acting social being. For it is the theory of the possible planning and arrangement of human labor."
— Martin Heidegger, *The End of Philosophy and the Task of Thinking*, 1966

"For all that, cybernetics is forced to acknowledge that, at least for the time being, a complete regulation of human existence is not yet possible. Consequently, in the universal domain of cybernetic science, the human being is still considered as a "source of irritation." What irritates in this sense is the apparent freedom of human plans and actions. Today, though, science has also taken possession of the field of human existence. It is undertaking the rigorously methodical exploration and planning of the possible future of active humanity. It calculates the information concerning that which the human being might have to face as to be planned."
—Martin Heidegger, *The Provenance of Art and the Destination of Thought*, 1967

In 1946 a conference of scientists was held in New York, with the object of extending the cybernetic hypothesis to the social sciences. The participants were united in support of an enlightened disqualification of the philistine philosophies of the social that focused on the individual or on society. *Sociocybernetics* must concentrate on the intermediary phenomena of *social feedback*, like those the American anthropological school thought it was discovering then between "culture" and "personality," in order to construct a characterology of nations intended for American soldiers. The operation consists in reducing dialectical thought to an observation of processes of *circular causality* within a social totality taken as invariant, combining contradiction and maladjustment as in the central category of cybernetic psychology, the *double bind*. As a science of society, cybernetics aims at inventing a social regulation that dispenses with macro-institutions—the State and the Market—in favor of micro-mechanisms of control, in favor of *apparatuses [dispositifs]*. The basic law of socio-cybernetics is the following: *growth and control increase/decrease inversely to each other.* So it's easier to construct a cybernetic social order on a small scale: "The rapid reestablishment of equilibria requires that the gaps be detected at the very places where the corrective action is carried out in a *decentralized way.*" Under the influence of Gregory Bateson—the Von Neumann of the social sciences—and the American sociological tradition obsessed by the question of deviance (the hobo, the immigrant, the criminal, the youth, I, you, he/she, etc.), socio-cybernetics prioritizes the study of *the individual as a locus of feedbacks*, that is, as a "self-disciplined personality." Bateson became the *chief social re-educator* of the second half of the 20th century, behind both the family therapy movement and the training in sales techniques that was developed at Palo Alto. For in fact the cybernetic hypothesis calls for a radically new structuring of the individual or collective subject, in the direction of a *hollowing-out*. It dismisses interiority as a myth and along with it the entire psychology of the 19th century, including psychoanalysis. It's no longer a matter of separating the subject from their traditional exter-nal ties as the liberal hypothesis had demanded, but of reconstructing the social bond by stripping the subject of any substance. Everyone must become *an envelope without flesh and blood*, the best possible conductor of social communication, the locus of an endless recursive loop that *rids itself of kinks*. In this way, the process of cybernetization completes the "civilizing process," with an abstracting of bodies and their affects into the regime of signs. "In this sense," writes Lyotard, "the system presents itself as the vanguardist machine that pulls humanity along after it, by dehumanizing it and then rehumanizing it at another level of normative capacity. Such is the hubris of the decision-makers, such is their blindness. [...] Even permissiveness with regard to the various games is placed under the condition of performativity. Redefining the norms of life consists in improving the system's proficiency as far as power is concerned."

Spurred on by the Cold War and its "witch hunts," the socio-cyberneticians search relentlessly for the pathological behind the normal, *the communist that lies dormant in everyone*. In the 1950s they form to this end the Federation of Mental Health Services where a *near-final* solution to the problems of community and of the epoch is spelled out: "It is the ultimate goal of mental health to help men live with their fellows in the same world... The concept of mental health is coextensive with the international order and the world community which must be developed in order that men may live in peace with one another." By rethinking mental disorders and social pathologies in terms of information, cybernetics founds a *new politics of subjects* based on communication, on transparency to oneself and to others. At the request of Bateson, Wiener in turn will begin to conceptualize a socio-cybernetics with a larger scope than improving mental health. He has no trouble explaining the failure of the liberal experiment: on the market, information is always impure and imperfect due at the same time to the deceitfulness of advertising, the monopolistic concentration of the media, and a misperception of States, which contain, as a collective, less information than civil society. The expansion of commodity relations, by increasing the size of communities, of feedback chains, makes distortions of communication and problems of social control even more probable. Not only was the social bond destroyed by the past process of accumulation but the social order appears impossible within capitalism. The good fortune of the cybernetic hypothesis is understandable, therefore, in light of the crises encountered by capitalism in the 20th century, which call into question the "laws" of classic political economy. It is this breach that the cybernetic discourse will rush to fill.

The contemporary history of the economic discourse should be considered from the angle of this *rise of the problem of information*. From the crisis of 1929 to 1949, the attention of economists focused on the questions of anticipation, of uncertainty connected with demand, of an adjustment between production and consumption, of projection of economic activity. The classic economics stemming from Adam Smith falters along with the other scientific discourses directly inspired by Newton's physics. The leading role that cybernetics will assume in economics after 1945 can be understood starting from an intuition by Marx, who observed that "in political economy, a law is determined by its opposite, the absence of laws. *The true law of political economy is chance.*" To prove that capitalism is not a factor of entropy and social chaos, economic discourse privileges, beginning in the 1940s, a redefinition of its psychology. It relies on the model of the "game theory" developed by Von Neumann and Oskar Morgenstern in 1944. The first socio-cyberneticians show that *homo economicus* could only exist on the condition of a *total transparency* of one's preferences to oneself and to others. Without the ability to know the whole set of behaviors of the other economic actors, the utilitarian idea of a rationality of micro-economic choices is only a fiction. Under the impetus of Friedrich von Hayek, the utilitarian paradigm was thus abandoned in favor of a theory of mechanisms of spontaneous coordination of individual choices, recognizing that each agent has only a limited knowledge of others' behaviors and of their own. The answer consists in sacrificing the autonomy of economic theory by grafting it onto the cybernetic promise of a balancing of systems. The resulting hybrid discourse, which came to be called "neo-liberal," attributes to the market virtues favoring an optimal allocation of information—*and no longer wealth*—in society. Thus, the market is the instrument of a perfect coordination of actors thanks to which the social totality achieves a lasting equilibrium. Here capitalism becomes incontestable insofar as it is presented as simply a means, the best means, *for producing social self-regulation.*

As in 1929, the global oppositional movement of 1968 and, even more so, the post-1973 crisis confronted the political economy with the problem of uncertainty once again, on an existential and political terrain this time. People get intoxicated by overblown theories, here that old windbag Edgar Morin with his "complexity," there Joël Rosnay, that enlightened simpleton, and his "society in real time." Ecological philosophy feeds on the new mystique of the "Big Everything." Nowadays, the totality is no longer an origin to be rediscovered but a future to be constructed. *The problem of cybernetics is no longer forecasting the future but reproducing the present.* It is no longer a question of a static order but of a dynamics of self-organization. Individuals are no longer credited with any power: their knowledge of the world is deficient, their desires are unknown to them, they are a mystery to themselves, everything eludes them, so that they are spontaneously cooperative, naturally empathetic, fatally united. They don't know anything about any of that, but everything is known about them. What we are seeing in process is the most advanced form of contemporary individualism, onto which is grafted the Hayekian philosophy for which every uncertainty, every possibility of an event is only a temporary lack of knowledge. Converted into an ideology, liberalism serves as a cover for a new collection of technical and scientific practices, a diffuse "second-order cybernetics," which deliberately blanks out its Christian name. Since the 1960s the very term cybernetics has melted into hybrid other terms. Indeed, the splitting of the sciences no longer permits any theoretical unification: henceforth the unity of cybernetics is manifested practically by the world it configures on a daily basis. It is the tool by which capitalism has adjusted its capacity for disintegration to its quest for profits, and vice versa. A society threatened with constant decomposition can be mastered all the better as an information system, an autonomous "nervous system," is formed that will enable it to be piloted, according to those monkeys of the State, Simon Nora and Alain Minc in their report of 1978. What is now called the "New Economy," bringing under one label of cybernetic origin the panoply of transformations the Western countries have undergone over the past thirty years, is a panoply of new subjugations, a new solution to the practical problem of the social order and its future, that is, a *new political regime*.

Under the influence of *computerization*, the techniques for adjusting supply and demand, issuing from the period 1930–1970, were stripped down, refined, and decentralized. The image of the "invisible hand" is no longer a justifying fiction but the actual principle of the social production of society, as it is materialized in the procedures of the computer. The techniques of commodity and financial intermediation have been automated. The Internet makes it possible at the same time to know the preferences of the consumer and to condition them through advertising. At another level, all the information on the behaviors of economic agents circulates in the form of assets [*titres*] handled by the financial markets. Each participant in capitalist valorization is the medium for near-continuous feedback loops in real time. On real markets and virtual markets alike, each transaction now gives rise to a circulation of information on the subjects and objects of exchange that goes beyond price setting, which has become secondary.

On the one hand, there is now an awareness of the importance of information as a factor of production distinct from labor and capital and decisive for "growth" in the form of knowledge, technical innovations, distributed competencies. On the other, the specialized sector of information production has continued to increase its size. Given the reciprocal reinforcement of these two tendencies, present-day capitalism can be considered as an *information economy*. Information has become a wealth to be extracted and accumulated, transforming capitalism into an *auxiliary* of cybernetics. The relation between capitalism and cybernetics inverted as the century progressed: while after the crisis of 1929, THEY constructed an information system upon economic activity in order to serve regulation—this was the objective of all the planning—the economy after the crisis of 1973 made the process of social self-regulation dependent on the valorization of information.

Nothing expresses the contemporary victory of cybernetics better than the fact that value can be extracted as *information about information*. Cybernetic-commodity logic, or "neoliberal" logic, extends to every activity, including not-yet market activity, with the unwavering support of the modern States. More generally, the precarization of capitalism's objects and subjects has as its corollary an increasing circulation of information about them: this is just as true of the worker, employed or unemployed, as it is of the common cow. *Consequently, cybernetics aims at disturbing and controlling in the same movement.* It is based on *terror* as a factor of development—of economic growth, or moral progress—because the terror furnishes the occasion for a production of information. The *state of emergency*, which is a characteristic feature of crises, is what gives a new impetus to self-regulation, enabling it to maintain itself as a perpetual motion. So that contrary to the schema of classic economics where the equilibrium of supply and demand should enable growth and thereby provide for the collective well-being, it is now "growth" that is an unrestricted path to equilibrium. So it is right to criticize Western modernity as a process of "endless mobilization" whose purpose is "movement toward more movement." But from a cybernetic viewpoint the self-production that characterizes the State and the Market as well as the automaton, the employee or the unemployed worker, is indiscernible from the self-control that tempers it and slows it down.

IV

"If motorized machines constituted the second age of the technical machine, cybernetic and informational machines form a third age that reconstructs a generalized regime of subjection: recurrent and reversible "humans-machines systems" replace the old nonrecurrent and nonreversible relations between the two elements; the relation between human and machine is based on internal, mutual communication, and no longer on usage or action. In the organic composition of capital, variable capital defines a regime of subjection of the worker (human surplus value), the principal framework of which is the business or factory. But with automation comes the progressive increase in the proportion of constant capital; we then see a new kind of enslavement at the same time the work regime changes, surplus value becomes machinic, and the framework expands to all of society. It could also be said that a small amount of subjectification took us away from machinic enslavement, but a large amount brings us back to it."
— Gilles Deleuze, Félix Guattari, *A Thousand Plateaus*, 1980

"The only moment of a class as such with any consistency is also the one that possesses its consciousness for itself: the class of managers of capital as a social machine. *The consciousness that connotes this class with the greatest coherence is that of apocalypse, of self-destruction."*
— Giorgio Cesarano, *Manuel de Survie*, 1975

It's clear, then, that cybernetics is not simply one of the aspects of contemporary life, its nanotechnological part for example, but the starting point and the arrival point of the new capitalism. *Cybernetic capitalism*—what does that mean? It means that since the 1970s we face an emergent social formation that is taking over from Fordist capitalism and that results from the application of the cybernetic hypothesis to political economy. Cybernetic capitalism develops in order to enable the society devastated by Capital to re-form and offer itself for a further cycle to the process of accumulation. On the one hand capitalism must grow, which implies a destruction. On the other it must reconstruct a semblance of the "human community," which implies a circulation. "There are," writes Lyotard, "two uses of wealth, that is to say of force-power [*puissance-pouvoir*]: a reproductive use and a plundering use. The first is circular, global, organic; the second is partial, deadly, jealous. [...] The capitalist is a conqueror and the conqueror is a monster, *a centaur*: its forequarters are nourished by the reproduction of regulated systems of metamorphoses controlled under the law of the commodity standard, and its hindquarters by looting overexcited energies. With one hand he appropriates, therefore retains, that is to say reproduces within equivalence, reinvests; with the other, he takes and destroys, steals and flees, hollowing out another space, another time." Capitalism's crises as Marx understood them always come from a disarticulation between the time of conquest and the time of reproduction. The function of cybernetics is to avoid these crises by ensuring the coordination between the "forequarters" and "hindquarters" of Capital. Its development is an endogenous response given to the problem posed by capitalism, which is *to develop without fatal disequilibria.*

In the logic of Capital, the development of the piloting function, the "control" function, corresponds to the subordination of the sphere of accumulation to the sphere of circulation. For the critique of political economy, circulation should not be less suspect, in fact, than production. As Marx knew, it's only a particular case of production taken in the general sense. The socialization of the economy—that is, the interdependence between the capitalists and the other members of the social body, the "human community"—the broadening of the human base of Capital, means that the extraction of surplus value, on which profit depends, is no longer centered on the relation of expropriation instituted by wage labor. Valorization's center of gravity shifts towards the sphere of circulation. Despite an inability to tighten the conditions of exploitation, which would bring about a crisis of consumption, capitalist accumulation can continue nonetheless, provided that the production-consumption cycle accelerates, that is, as long as the process of production and commodity circulation both accelerate. What was lost at the static level of the economy can be made up for at the dynamic level. The logic of flows will dominate the logic of the end product. Speed will take precedence over quantity, as a factor of wealth. *The hidden side of the maintenance of accumulation is the acceleration of circulation.* The control apparatuses will have the function, consequently, of maximizing the volume of commodity flows while minimizing the events, obstacles, accidents that would slow them down. Cybernetic capitalism tends to abolish time itself, to maximize fluid circulation to its limit point, the speed of light, a point that certain financial transactions are already approaching. The categories of "real time" and "just-in-time" attest rather clearly to this *aversion to duration*. For this very reason, time is our ally.

This propensity to control on the part of capitalism is not new. It is postmodern only in the sense where postmodernity merges with modernity in its last phase. It is for this very reason that bureaucracy was developed at the end of the 19th century and information technologies after the Second World War. The cybernetization of capitalism began at the end of the 1870s with an increasing control of production, distribution, and consumption. It was then that information on the flows assumed a central strategic importance as a condition of valorization. The historian James Beniger relates that the first problems of control appeared when the first collisions between trains occurred, imperiling commodities as well as human lives. Railway signaling and devices for measuring travel times and transmitting data had to be invented to avert such "catastrophes." The telegraph, synchronized clocks, flow charts in the big corporations, weighing systems, road maps, performance evaluation procedures, wholesaling, the assembly line, centralized decision making, catalogue advertising, and mass communication media were invented during this period in response to a generalized crisis of control in every economic sphere, linked to the acceleration of production precipitated by the industrial revolution in the United States. So information and control systems developed as the capitalist process of transformation of material expanded. A class of intermediaries, of *middlemen* that Alfred Chandler called the "invisible hand" of

Capital, formed and grew. Starting at the end of the 19th century, it was noted that *predictability was becoming a source of profit seeing that it was a source of confidence*. Fordism and Taylorism were part of this movement, as was the development of control over the mass of consumers and control of public opinion through marketing and advertising, charged with forcibly *extorting*, then putting to work, the "preferences" that, according to the hypothesis of the economic marginalists, are the true source of value. Investment in the technologies of planning and control—organizational or purely technical—became more and more profitable. After 1945, cybernetics supplied capitalism with a new infrastructure of machines—computers—and more importantly with an intellectual technology that made it possible to regulate the circulation of flows in society, making them *exclusively commodity flows*.

The fact that the economic sector of information, communication, and control played an increasing part in economy from the Industrial Revolution onward, that "immaterial labor" grew compared to material labor, has nothing surprising about it therefore. Today in industrialized countries it mobilizes more than two thirds of the labor capacity. But this is not enough for defining cybernetic capitalism. The latter, because it *continuously* makes its equilibrium and its growth depend on its control capabilities, has *changed its nature. Insecurity, much more so than scarcity, is the kink in present-day capitalism.* As Wittgenstein realized on the basis of the crisis of 1929, and Keynes in his wake—there is a very strong connection between the "state of confidence" and the curve of marginal efficiency of Capital, writes Keynes in Chapter 12 of the *General Theory* in February 1934—the economy ultimately rests on a "language game." The markets, and with them the commodities and the sellers, the sphere of circulation in general, and consequently, the company, the sphere of production as the site where future yields are projected, do not exist without conventions, social norms, technical standards, truth standards, a meta-level that causes bodies and things to exist as commodities, even before they become the object of a price. The sectors of control and communication develop because commodity valorization requires the organization of a closed loop of information circulation, parallel with the circulation of commodities, the production of a collective belief that is objectified in value. For it to occur, an exchange needs "investments of form"—a *reliable* information about, and a shaping *of*, the thing that is exchanged—a *formatting* that makes it possible to establish equivalence before the exchange has actually taken place, a conditioning that is also a precondition of the agreement on the market. This is true for goods; it's also true for persons. To perfect the circulation of information will be to perfect the market as a universal instrument of coordination. Contrary to what the liberal hypothesis supposed, in order to prop up a fragile capitalism the contract in social relations does not suffice in itself. THEY realize after 1929 that any contract must be combined with controls. The entry of cybernetics into the operation of capitalism aims at minimizing the uncertainties, the incommensurabilities, the expectation problems that might interfere with any commodity transaction. It contributes to consolidating the basis on which capitalism's mechanisms can function, to oiling the abstract machine of Capital.

With cybernetic capitalism, the *political moment* of political economy thus dominates its economic moment. Or as Joan Robinson understands it, commenting on Keynes and his economic theory: "As soon as the uncertainty of expectations that guide economic behavior is admitted, equilibrium drops out of the argument and history takes its place." The political moment, understood here in the broad sense as that which subjugates, normalizes, determines what passes through bodies and can be registered as socially recognized value, as what extracts forms-of-life from form, is essential to "growth" and to the reproduction of the system: on the one hand the appropriation of energies, their orientation, their crystallization, becomes the primary source of valorization; on the other, the surplus value can come from whatever point of the bio-political fabric as long as the latter ceaselessly reconstitutes itself. That all the expenditures tend to morph into valorizable qualities also signifies that Capital permeates all living flows: socialization of the economy and anthropomorphosis of Capital are two conjoined and indissociable processes. For them to be realized, it is necessary and sufficient that every contingent action be taken into a mix of *surveillance and capture* apparatuses. The first draw their inspiration from prison insofar as it introduces a regime of panoptic, centralized visibility. They have long been a monopoly of the modern State. The second are inspired by information technology insofar as it aims at a regime of decentralized mapping-and-control [*quadrillage*] in real time. The shared horizon of these apparatuses is that of a *total transparency*, an absolute correspondence between the map and the territory, a will to know to such a degree of accumulation that it becomes a will to power. One of the advances of cybernetics has consisted in fencing off systems of surveillance and monitoring while ensuring that the surveillants and the monitors are surveilled and monitored in their turn, and this in accordance with a *socialization of control* that is the hallmark of the so-called "information society." The control sector tends toward autonomy because of *the need to control the control*, the commodity flow being accompanied by information flows whose circulation and security must be optimized in turn. At the summit of this layering of controls, State control, the police and the law, legitimate violence and judicial power play a role of *ultimate controllers*. Regarding this surveillance build-up that characterizes "control societies," Deleuze explains it simply: such societies "are full of holes—things are escaping all over the place." Which confirms time and again the need for control. "In the disciplinary societies one was always starting again (from school to the barracks, from the barracks to the factory), while in the societies of control one is never done with anything."

So there is nothing surprising in seeing the development of cybernetic capitalism accompanied by a development of every form of repression, by an *extreme securitarianism*. Traditional discipline and the generalization of the state of emergency, of the *emergenza*, are given new life in a system entirely turned toward *the fear of threat*. The apparent contradiction between a strengthening of the State's repressive functions and a neoliberal economic discourse that advocates "less State intervention"—

which for example allows Löic Wacquant to launch into a critique of liberal ideology that ignores the rise of the "penal State"—can only be understood by reference to the cybernetic hypothesis. Lyotard explains the matter: "There is in every cybernetic system a unit of reference which allows the disparity produced by the introduction of an event into the system to be measured; then, thanks to this measure, this event can be translated into information for the system. Finally, if it is a matter of a homeostatically regulated whole, this disparity can be annulled and the system led back to the same quantity of energy or information that it had previously. [...] Let's stop here for a moment. We see how the adoption of this perspective on society, that is, the despotic phantasy of the master situated on the alleged site of the central zero and hence identifying himself with the matrix of the Nothing [...] can only compel him to extend his idea of the threat and therefore of defense. *For what event does not present any danger from this perspective?* Not one; quite the contrary, since they are disturbances of a circular order, reproducing the same, requiring energy to be expended for purposes of appropriation and elimination. Is this too abstract? Do we need an example? It is the same project as perpetuates, in France and in high places, the institution of an operational Defense of the territory, secured from an operational Center of the infantry, whose specialty is to stave off the 'internal' threat, originating from dark corners of the social body, whose administrative staff claim nothing less than to be a clairvoyant head: this clairvoyance is called the national register; [...] the translation of the event into information for the system is called intelligence [...] finally the execution of regulatory orders and their inscription on the 'social body,' especially when one imagines this as subject to some intense emotion, for example, the fear and panic that shake it up in every sense and in the case where a nuclear war might be set off (meaning also: where there arises some upsurge or other of protest, contestation, or civil disobedience, regarded as insane)—this execution requires the assiduous and subtle infiltration of the communication channels into the social 'flesh,' as a certain superior officer marvelously put it, 'the *policing of spontaneous movements.*'" Prison is thus at the top of a cascade of control apparatuses, the final guarantee that no disruptive incident will take place in the social body to hinder the circulation of persons and goods. The logic of cybernetics being to replace centralized institutions, sedentary forms of control, with tracking tools, nomadic forms of control, prison as a classic apparatus of surveillance is obviously being expanded by capture devices like the electronic bracelet, for example.

The development of "community policing" in the Anglo-Saxon world, of "*police de proximité*" in France, also answers to a cybernetic logic aimed at warding off the event, at organizing feedback. According to this logic, disruptions in a zone will be stifled all the more effectively as they will be absorbed by the closest sub-zones of the system.

If repression has the role, in cybernetic capitalism, of forestalling the event, prediction is its corollary, insofar as it is for the purpose of eliminating the uncertainty that's associated with any future. It is the major concern of the statistical technologies. Whereas those of the welfare State were completely focused on the anticipation of risks, calculated or not, those of cybernetic capitalism aim at multiplying the domains of responsibility. The discourse concerning risk is the driver for deploying the cybernetic hypothesis; it is circulated first and then internalized. Because risks are more easily accepted if those exposed to them have the impression they have chosen to take them, feel responsible for them and, furthermore, feel that they have the power to control and master them themselves. But, as one expert admits, "zero risk" does not exist: "The notion of risk does weaken causal links, but in doing so it does not make them disappear. On the contrary it multiplies them. [...] To consider a danger in terms of risk is necessarily to admit that one can never shield oneself from it absolutely: one can manage it, domesticate it, but never wipe it out." By virtue of its permanence for the system, risk is an ideal tool for promoting new forms of power that favor the increasing hold of security apparatuses on collectives and individuals. It eliminates any question of conflict by the obligatory drawing together of individuals around the management of threats that are supposed to concern everyone in the same way. The argument that THEY want us to accept is the following: greater security goes hand in hand with an increased production of insecurity. And if you think that the insecurity increases as prediction tends to be infallible, that's because you are yourself afraid of risks. And if you are afraid of risks, if you don't trust the system to completely control your life, your fear risks being contagious and in fact may present a very real risk of disloyalty to the system. In other words, to be afraid of risks is already to be seen as a risk to society oneself. The imperative of commodity circulation on which cybernetic capitalism is based morphs into a general phobia, a fantasy of self-destruction. The control society is a paranoiac society, something that is clearly confirmed by the proliferation of conspiracy theories within it. Thus every individual is subjectified in cybernetic capitalism as a *risky dividual*, as the *generic enemy* of the balanced society.

So it shouldn't be a surprise when the reasoning of Capital's collaborators-in-chief in France, François Ewald and Denis Kessler, leads them to assert that by reducing the social risks, the welfare State, characteristic of the Fordist mode of social regulation, ended up depriving individuals of their sense of responsibility. The dismantling of the systems of social protection that we are witnessing since the beginning of the eighties, aims consequently at restoring everyone's sense of responsibility by making them *all* bear the "risks" that capitalists alone impose on the whole "social body." In the last analysis, it's a matter of instilling the point of view of social reproduction in each individual, who should no longer expect anything from society but sacrifice everything to it. Because the social regulation of catastrophes and of the unforeseen can no longer be managed, as it was in the Middle Ages, solely by social exclusion, scapegoating, restraints, and enclosure. If everyone must become responsible for the risk they make society incur, this is because one can no longer exclude without depriving oneself of a potential source of profit. Cybernetic capitalism thus couples a socialization of the economy with a rise of the "responsibility principle." It produces the citizen as a "risky dividual" who self-neutralizes their potential for the destruction of order. In this way, it's a matter of generalizing automatic control, an arrangement that favors the proliferation of apparatuses. *Every crisis, in cybernetic capitalism, signals a reinforcement of apparatuses.* The anti-GMO contestation as well as the "mad cow crisis" of these past few years in France, ultimately made it possible to establish an unprecedented traceability of dividuals and things. The increased professionalization of control—which along with insurance is one of the economic sectors whose growth is guaranteed by the cybernetic logic—is just the other side of the rise of the citizen, as a political subjectivity having self-repressed the risk it objectively represents. Citizen vigilance contributes in this way to the improvement of piloting apparatuses.

Whereas the upsurge of control at the end of the 19th century was predicated on a dissolution of personal ties—so that THEY were able to speak of a "disappearance of communities"—in cybernetic capitalism it was achieved through a new weaving together of social ties completely imbued with the imperative of piloting oneself and others in the service of social unity: it is this *becoming-apparatus* of humanity that the citizen of Empire represents. The current importance of these new *citizen-apparatus systems*, which are hollowing out the old State institutions and propelling the citizen-communitarian nebula, demonstrates that the great social machine that cybernetic capitalism is meant to be cannot do without men and women, although certain skeptical cyberneticians took some time to admit this, as is evidenced by this peeved realization from the mid-1980s:

"Systematic automation would indeed be a radical means of overcoming the physical or mental limits that are responsible for the most common human errors: momentary loss of vigilance due to fatigue, stress, or routine; temporary inability to interpret simultaneously a welter of contradictory information and hence to master overly complex situations; euphemization of the risk under the pressure of circumstances (emergencies, hierachical pressures...); errors of representation leading one to overestimate the security of normally very reliable systems (people cite the case of a pilot who refuses categorically to believe that one of his engines is on fire). One has to wonder, however, if removing man from the circuit—regarding him as the weak link of the man/machine interface—does not ultimately risk creating new vulnerabilities, if only by increasing the errors of representation and losses of vigilance that are, as we have seen, the frequent result of an exaggerated sense of security. In any case the debate merits being opened."

Indeed.

V

"Ecosociety is decentralized, communitarian, participatory. Individual responsibility and initiative really exist. Ecosociety is based on the pluralism of ideas, styles and behaviors of life. Consequently, equality and social justice are in progress. But also, there are changes in customs, ways of thinking, and norms. Men have invented a different life in a society in equilibrium. They realized that maintaining a state of equilibrium was a more delicate matter than maintaining a state of continuous growth. Thanks to a new vision, a new logic of complementarity, new values, the men of ecosociety have invented an economic doctrine, a political science, a sociology, a technology, and a psychology of the state of controlled equilibrium."
— Joël de Rosnay, *Le Macroscope*, 1975

Capitalism and socialism represent two organizations of the economy derived from the same basic system, that of the quantification of added value [...] Considered from this angle, the system called "socialism" is only the corrective sub-system applied to "capitalism." Thus we can also say that the most radical capitalism is socialist in certain of its aspects, and that socialism as a whole is a "mutation"

of capitalism designed to try and stabilize the system through a redistribution, a distribution thought to be necessary for ensuring the survival of everyone and to spur them towards a broader consumption. In this sketch we will call "social capitalism" an organization of the economy conceived with the aim of establishing an acceptable balance between capitalism and socialism."
— Yona Friedman, *Utopies réalisables*, 1974

The events of May 68 provoked in all the Western societies a political reaction whose scope THEY have trouble recalling today. In short order, a restructuring of capitalism was organized, *in the way an army is mobilized*. One saw, with the Club of Rome, multinationals like Fiat, Volkswagen, and Ford pay economists, sociologists, and ecologists to determine the kinds of production that companies should discontinue in order for the capitalist system to function better and become stronger. In 1972, a report from the Massachusetts Institute of Technology, *Limits to Growth*, commissioned by the said "club," created a big stir because it recommended halting the capitalist accumulation process, including in the so-called developing countries. From the top tier of social domination, THEY called for "zero growth" in the interest of preserving social relations and the resources of the planet. THEY introduced qualitative components in the analysis of development that were incompatible with the quantitative projections centered on growth. They ultimately demanded that the latter be completely redefined and this pressure was accentuated when the crisis of 1973 broke out. Capitalism seemed to be conducting its own auto-critique. But if I have spoken again of war and armies, it's because the MIT report, written by the economist Dennis H. Meadows, drew inspiration from the work of a certain Jay Forrester who had been commissioned in 1952 by the U.S. Air force to develop a system of alert and defense—the SAGE SYSTEM—that would coordinate for the first time radar devices and computers for the purpose of detecting and thwarting a possible attack on American territory by enemy rockets. Forrester had mounted infrastructures of communication and control between men and machines where the latter were interconnected in "real time" for the first time. Then he was hired in the MIT's school of management to share his expertise in system analysis with the economic world. He applied the same principles of order and defense to the cor-porations, then to the cities, and finally to the entire planet in his work, *World Dynamics*, which inspired the reporters of MIT In this way, "second-order cybernetics" was decisive for determining the principles of the restructuring of capitalism. With it, political economy became *a science of the living*. It analyzed the world as an open system of transformation and circulation of energy flows and monetary flows.

In France a group of pseudo-savants—the enlightened idiot de Rosnay and the blowhard Morin but also the mystic Henri Atlan, Henri Laborit, René Passet, and the arriviste Attali— got together to formulate, in the wake of MIT, *Ten Command-ments for a New Economy,* an "eco-socialism" they claimed, by using a systemic, which is to say a cybernetic, approach obsessed by the "state of equilibrium" of everything and everybody. It may be worthwhile *a posteriori,* when one listens to today's left as well as the "left of the left," to recall some of the principles that de Rosnay presented in 1975:

1. Preserve the variety of our spaces and cultures, biodiversity as well as multiculturality.
2. Take care not to open up, not to let leak, information contained in the cycles of regulation.
3. Reestablish the equilibria of the whole system by means of decentralization.
4. Differentiate so as to better integrate, for as the most enlightened of all the cyberneticians, Teilhard de Chardin, intuited, "every real integration is based on a prior differentiation. [...] The homogeneous, the mélange, the syncretic, is entropy. Only *union in diversity* is creative. It increases complexity, it leads to higher levels of organization."
5. Develop: allow yourself to be aggressive.

6. Prefer objectives, *projects* with detailed programming.
7. Know how to use information.
8. Know how to maintain constraints on the elements of the system.

It's no longer a matter, as THEY could still pretend to believe in 1972, of calling capitalism and its devastating effects into question, but rather of "*reorienting* the economy so that it better serves, at the same time, human needs, the maintenance and development of the social system, and the pursuit of a true cooperation with nature. The equilibrium economy characterizing the eco-society is therefore a 'regulated' economy in the cybernetic sense of the term." The first ideologues of cybernetic capitalism talked about opening up capitalism to a communitarian management *from below*, to an empowerment of everyone thanks to the "collective intelligence" that would result from progress in telecommunications and information technology. Without calling private property, or State property, back into question, THEY invited "people" to join in a co-management, a control of the corporations by communities of wage earners and users. The cybernetic reformative euphoria was such that, at the beginning of the 1970s, THEY evoked without shuddering, as if it had been a question of anything else since the 19th century, the idea of a "social capitalism," of the sort defended for example by the ecologist architect and compulsive writer Yona Friedman. Thus there took form something THEY would end up calling "socialism of the third way" and its alliance with ecology, whose current political hold on Europe is well known, we're told. If one had to name one event that, in those years in France, exposed the tortuous progression toward this new alliance between socialism and liberalism, not without the hope that something different would emerge, it would be, without question, the LIP affair. With it, all of socialism, including its most radical currents such as "council communism," failed to bring down the liberal setup, and without suffering a defeat, strictly speaking. It has simply ended up being absorbed by cybernetic capitalism. The recent adherence of the ecologist Cohn-Bendit, the good-hearted leader of May 68, to the liberal-libertarian current is only one logical consequence of the deeper turning of "socialist ideas" back upon themselves.

The current "anti-globalization movement" and the citizen-based contestation in general don't present any break within this formation of statements elaborated thirty years ago. They simply demand an acceleration of its practical application. Behind the noisy counter-summits, one recognizes the same cold vision of society as a totality threatened with explosions, the same *objective of social regulation*. It's a matter of *restoring* a social cohesion pulverized by the dynamic of cybernetic capitalism and of ultimately *guaranteeing* everyone's participation in that dynamic. So it is not surprising to see the most arid economism spread so tenaciously and nauseatingly through the ranks of the citizenry. The citizen dispossessed of everything projects themself as an *amateur* expert in social management and sees the nothingness of their life as an unbroken succession of projects to be realized. As the sociologist Luc Boltanski remarks with a feigned naivety, "everything can attain the dignity of the *project*, including endeavors that are hostile to capitalism." Just as the "self-management" construct was seminal in the reorganization of capitalism over the past thirty years, citizen action is nothing other than the current instrument of the modernization of politics. This new "civilizing process" is based on the critique of authority developed in the 1970s, when second-order cybernetics was crystallizing. The critique of political representation as a separate power, already recuperated by the new management in the sphere of economic production, is now being reinvested in the political sphere. Everywhere you look it's all about the horizontality of relations of participation in projects that are meant to replace the old-fashioned hierarchical and bureaucratic authority, counterpowers and decentralizations that are supposed to undo the monopolies and the secrecy. In this way the chains of social interdependence are extended and tightened without hindrance; here they're made of surveillance, elsewhere of delegation. The integration of civil society by the State and the integration of the State by civil society mesh together more and more smoothly. In this way *the division of labor for the management of populations* is organized, an organization necessary to the dynamic of cybernetic capitalism. In the foreseeable future, the affirmation of a "world citizenship" will complete the process.

The fact is that starting in the 1970s, socialism has become nothing but a democratism, absolutely necessary now to the advancement of the cybernetic hypothesis. The ideal of direct democracy, of participatory democracy, must be understood as the desire for a general expropriation by the cybernetic system of *all the information* contained in its parts. The demand for transparency, for traceability, is the demand for a perfect circulation of information, a *progressivism in the logic of flows* that governs cybernetic capitalism. Between 1965 and 1970 a young German philosopher, the presumed heir of "critical theory," established the democratic paradigm of current contestation by instigating several controversies with his elders.

Against the socio-cybernetician Niklas Luhmann, a hyper-functionalist theoretician of systems, Habermas cited the unpredictability of dialogue, of argumentation, which could not be reduced simply to exchanges of information. But it was especially against Marcuse that he laid out the project of a generalized "discourse ethics" that would critically radicalize the democratic project of the Enlightenment. To Marcuse, who explained, commenting on the observations of Max Weber, that "rationalization" means that technical reason, at the basis of industrialization and capitalism, is a political reason at its core, Habermas shot back that a set of immediate intersubjective relations escapes subject-object relations mediated by technical logic and that ultimately they frame them and orient them. In other words, faced with the development of the cybernetic hypothesis, politics should aim at autonomizing and expanding this sphere of discourses, at multiplying the democratic arenas, at constructing and seeking a consensus that, by its very nature, would be emancipatory. In addition to reducing the "lived world," "everyday life," all that escapes the social control machine, to social interactions, to discourses, at a deeper level Habermas fails to consider the fundamental heterogeneity of forms-of-life in relation to each other. Just like the contract, consensus is attached to the objective of unification and pacification through the management of differences. In the cybernetic framework, any faith in "communicational action," any communication that doesn't assume the impossibility of its possibility, ends up serving control. That is why technology and science are not simply, as Habermas thinks, ideologies that overlay the concrete fabric of intersubjective relations. They are "materialized ideologies," cascading apparatuses, a concrete governmentality that pervades those relations. We don't want more transparency or more democracy. There is quite enough of both. On the contrary, we want more opacity and more intensity.

But I will not have finished with socialism as it has been consigned to obsolescence by the cybernetic hypothesis until I've evoked another voice: I have to say something about the criticism centered on the men-machines relationship that since the 1970s has addressed the supposed crux of the problem by raising the question of technology beyond technophobia—that of a Theodore Kaczynski or the educated monkey from Oregon, John Zerzan—and technophilia, and that aims to found a new *radical ecology* that is not simply Romantic. As early as the economic crisis of the 1970s, Ivan Illich was among the first to express the hope of a revamping of social practices not just through a new relationship between subjects, as in

Habermas, but also between subjects and objects, through a "re-appropriation of tools" and institutions that would result from a general "conviviality"; a conviviality that would be capable of undermining the law of value. The philosopher of technics, Simondon, even sees this re-appropriation as the lever for surpassing Marx and Marxism: "Labor possesses an intelligence of the elements, capital possesses an intelligence of ensembles; but it's not by joining together an intelligence of the elements and an intelligence of ensembles that the intermediary and unmixed intelligence that constitutes the technical individual can be created. [...] The dialogue of capital and labor is false because it is a thing of the past. Collectivization of the means of production cannot bring about a reduction in alienation by itself; it can bring it about only if it is the precondition of the acquisition by the human individual of an intelligence of the individuated technical object. This relation of the human individual to the technical individual is the most delicate relation to form." The solution to the problem of political economy, of capitalist alienation, and of cybernetics would reside in the invention of a new relation to machines, a "technical culture" that is said to have been lacking in Western modernity thus far. It is just such a doctrine that accounts for the massive development, over the past thirty years, of "citizen" education in the sciences and technology. Since living beings, contrary to what the cybernetic hypothesis assumes, are essentially *different* from machines, man has a responsibility to *represent* technical objects: "Man as witness of the machines," writes Simondon, "is responsible for their relation: the individual machine represents man, but man represents the whole array of machines, for there is no one machine of all the machines, whereas there can be a thought concerned with all the machines." In its present utopian form, as in Guattari at the end of his life or today in Bruno Latour, this school will claim to *make objects speak*, to represent their norms in the public arena through a "parliament of things." Eventually the technocrats would have to give way to "mechanologists" and other "mediologists" about whom one doesn't see how they would differ from the current technocrats unless it's in their being more adapted to technical life, citizens ideally wedded to their apparatuses. What our utopians pretend not to realize is that the integration of technical rationality by everyone would not alter the existing power relations in any significant way. Recognition of the men-machines hybridism of social assemblages would almost certainly extend the struggle for recognition and the tyranny of transparency to the inanimate world. In this renovated political ecology, socialism and cybernetics attain their optimal point of convergence: the project of a green

Republic, a *technical democracy*—"a renewal of democracy could have as its objective a pluralist management of all its machinic components," writes Guattari in his last published text—the deadly vision of a definitive peace between humans and non-humans.

VI

"Just as modernization did in a previous era, post-modernization or informatization today marks a new mode of becoming human. Where the production of soul is concerned, as Musil would say, one really ought to replace the traditional techniques of industrial machines with the cybernetic intelligence of information and communication technologies. We must invent what Pierre Lévy calls an 'anthropology of cyberspace.'"
— Michael Hardt, Toni Negri, *Empire*, 1999

"Communication is the third fundamental medium of imperial control. [...] The contemporary systems of communication are not subordinated to sovereignty; on the contrary, sovereignty seems to be subordinated to communication. [...] Communication is the form of capitalist production in which capital has succeeded in submitting society entirely and globally to its regime, suppressing all alternative paths."
— Michael Hardt, Toni Negri, *Empire*, 1999

The cybernetic utopia did not just vampirize socialism and its oppositional power by turning it into a "kindred democratism." In those years full of confusion, the 1970s, it also contaminated the most advanced Marxism, making its perspective untenable and inoffensive. As Lyotard writes in 1979, "In one way or another, the critique of political economy and the critique of alienation that was its corollary are everywhere being used as elements *in the programming of the system*." Opposite the unifying cybernetic hypothesis, the *abstract* axiom of potentially revolutionary antagonism—class struggle, human community (*Gemeinwesen*), or "social living" [*social-vivant*] against Capital, general intellect against exploitation process, "multitude" against "Empire," "creativity" or "virtuosity" against labor, "social wealth" against commodity value, etc.—ultimately serves the political project of a greater social integration. The critique of political economy or ecology don't critique the type of economy that characterizes capitalism or the totalizing and systemic vision that characterizes cybernetics. Paradoxically, they even make these into the drivers of their emancipatory philosophies of history. Their teleology is no longer that of the proletariat or of nature, but that of Capital. Nowadays their perspective is fundamentally that of a social economy, a "solidarity economy," a "transformation of the mode of production," no longer through a collectivization or nationalization of the means of production but through a *collectivization of production decisions*. As a Yann Moulier-Boutang, for example, pitches the notion, it's a matter of "the collective, social character of wealth creation" finally being *recognized*, of the citizen's life as such being valorized. This "communism" boils down to an economic democratism, to the project of reconstructing a "post-Fordist" State from below. Social cooperation is posited as always-already given, without ethical incommensurabilities, without interferences with the circulation of affects, without problems of community.

Toni Negri's itinerary inside Autonomia, and then the gaggle of his disciples in France and in the Anglo-Saxon world, shows the extent to which Marxism authorized this kind of slide toward the will to will, an "endless mobilization," ensuring its eventual, inevitable, defeat by the cybernetic hypothesis. The latter didn't have any difficulty interfacing with the metaphysics of production that the whole of Marxism relies on and that Negri pushes to its limit by considering every affect, every emotion, every communication to be in the last analysis a piece of labor. From this viewpoint, autopoeisis, self-production, self-organization, and autonomy are categories that play a homologous role in the distinct discursive formations where they emerged. The demands inspired by this critique of political economy, that of the guaranteed income as well as that of "documentation for everyone" only address the basic reality of the sphere of production. If some of those who are asking for a guaranteed income have been able to break with the perspective of full employment—that is, with the belief in work as a fundamental value—that still predominated in the previous movements of the unemployed, this has been, paradoxically, while preserving an inherited, restrictive definition of value as "labor value." In this way they can overlook the fact that in the end they are helping to improve the circulation of goods and persons.

Now it's precisely because valorization is no longer assignable in the last instance to what goes on in the sphere of production alone that henceforth the political gesture—I'm thinking of the strike, for example, to say nothing of the general strike— must be shifted toward the spheres of circulation of products and information. Who doesn't see that the demand for "documentation for everyone," if it is satisfied, will only contribute to a greater mobility of labor power at the global level, something that liberal American thinkers have well understood? As for the guaranteed wage, if it were obtained wouldn't it just introduce an additional revenue into the circuit of value? It would represent the formal equivalent of an investment by the system in its "human capital," a credit: it would anticipate a production to come. In the context of the present restructuring of capital, calling for it could be compared to a neo-Keynesian proposal for rekindling the "effective demand" that can serve as a safety net for the desired development of the "New Economy." Whence also the support of several economists for the idea of a "universal income" or "citizenship income." What would justify the latter, including in the opinion of Negri and his followers, is seeing it as a *social debt contracted* by capitalism to the "multitude." And if I said earlier that Negri's Marxism had functioned, like all the other Marxisms, on the basis of an *abstract* axiom concerning social antagonism, it's because it *concretely* needs the fiction of the unity of the social body. In its most aggressive offensives, such as the movement of the unemployed during the winter of 1997–1998, its perspectives still aim at instituting a *new social contract*, call it communist or not. Within classic politics,

Negriism already plays the role of vanguard of the environmentalist movements.

To relocate the intellectual conjuncture that explains this blind faith in the social conceived as the possible object and subject of a contract, as an ensemble of equivalent elements, one has to go back to the end of the 1950s, when the gradual decomposition of the working class in Western societies troubled Marxist theoreticians because it invalidated the axiom of class warfare. Some of them thought they had discovered in Marx's *Grundrisse* an exposition, a prefiguration of what capitalism and its proletariat were in the process of becoming. In the "Fragment on Machines," Marx envisages that in full-blown industrialization individual labor capacity may cease to be the main source of surplus value because "general social knowledge" would become the direct force of production. That kind of capitalism, which today is called "cognitive capitalism," would no longer be contested by the proletariat that was born in the great factories. Marx imagines that it would be contested by the "social individual." He specifies the reason for this ineluctable process of overthrow: "Capital calls to life all the powers of science and of nature, as of social combination and of social intercourse, in order to make the creation of wealth independent (relatively) of the labor time employed in it [...] these are the material conditions to blow the foundation sky-high." The system's contradiction, its catastrophic antagonism, would come from the fact that Capital measures all value in labor time while being forced to diminish the latter because of the productivity gains that automation makes possible. Capitalism is doomed in sum because it demands less labor and more labor at the same time. The responses to the economic crises of the 1970s, the cycle of struggles that lasted more than ten years in Italy, give an unexpected boost to this teleology. The utopia of a world in which machines will work in our place appears to be within reach. Creativity, the social individual, the general intellect—student youth, cultivated marginals, cognitive workers, etc. —free of the relation of exploitation, would be the new subject of the coming communism. For some, Negri or Castoriadis among them, but also the Situationists, this means that the new revolutionary subject will re-appropriate his or her "creativity," or their "imaginary," confiscated by the labor relation, will make non-work time a new source of emancipation of oneself and of the collectivity. Autonomia as a political movement was to be based on these analyses.

In 1973, Lyotard, who frequented Castoriadis for a time inside of *Socialisme ou Barbarie*, notes the lack of differentiation between this new Marxist or post-Marxist discourse on the general intellect and the discourse concerning the new political economy: "the body of machines that you call the social subject and man's universal productive force is just the body of modern Capital. The knowledge in question here is not the property of all individuals, it is separate, a moment in the metamorphosis of capital, obeying the latter as much as governing it." The ethical problem posed by this hope placed in the collective intellect, which shows up today in the utopias featuring autonomous collective uses of communication networks, is the following: "one can't decide that the principal role of knowledge is to be an indispensable element in the functioning of society and thus to act on the latter's behalf, unless one has decided that society is a great machine. Conversely, one can't take its critical function into account and consider orienting its development and propagation in that direction unless one has decided it doesn't at all form an integrated whole and it remains haunted by a principle of contestation." By combining the two terms of this alternative, irreconcilable though they are, all the heterogeneous positions whose matrix we have found in the discourses of Toni Negri and his followers, and that represent the completion point of the Marxist tradition, are condemned to political aimlessness, to having no other destination than the one reserved for them by domination. Here the essential thing, which seduces so many intellectual apprentices, is that these knowledges [*savoirs*] are never powers [*pouvoirs*], that knowledge [*connaissance*] is never knowledge of oneself, that intelligence always remains separate from experience. The political technique of Negriism is to formalize the informal, to make explicit the implicit, make patent the tacit, in short to valorize what is *value-free*. And in fact, Negri's faithful dog, Yann Moulier-Boutang, in a surreal rant by a debilitated cocaine addict, let drop this bit of wisdom in 2005: "Capitalism in its new phase, or its last frontier, needs the communism of the multitudes." The *neutral communism* of Negri, the mobilization it calls for, is not only compatible with cybernetic capitalism, it is has become the necessary condition for the latter's implementation.

Once the proposals of the MIT report were digested, the economists of growth did underscore the vital role of creativity, of technological innovation—alongside the Capital and Labor factors—in the production of surplus value. And other experts, equally informed, then stated pedantically that the readiness to innovate depended on the population's degree of education, of training, of health—THEY would begin calling this "human capital," following Gary Becker, the most radical of the economistic thinkers—and on the synergy between economic agents—a synergy that can be fostered by establishing a regular circulation of information, by communication networks—as well as the synergy between activity and the environment, human life and non-human life. What would explain the crisis of the 1970s is that there is a cognitive and natural social base for maintaining and developing capitalism that was neglected up to then. At a deeper level, this means that non-work time, all the moments that escape the circuits of commodity valorization—which is to say, everyday life—are also a factor in growth, possessing a *potential value* insofar as they make it possible to maintain the human base of Capital. At that point in the discussion one saw armies of experts recommending that corporations apply cybernetic solutions to the organization of production: development of telecommunications, organization into networks, "participatory management" or on a project basis, panels of consumers and quality controls, would all contribute to bringing the profit rates back up. Consequently, for those who wanted to get out of the crisis of the 1970s without calling capitalism back into question, "rekindling growth," and no longer halting it, implied a deep reorganization in the direction of a democratization of economic choices and an institutional support of time for living, as in the demand for "freeness" [*gratuité*] for example. It is only in this sense that THEY can claim *today* that the "new spirit of capitalism" has inherited from the social critique of the years 1960-1970: to the precise extent that the cybernetic hypothesis inspired the mode of social regulation that emerged then.

So it is hardly surprising that communication, the placing in common of powerless forms of knowledge that cybernetics carries out, now authorizes the most advanced ideologues such as Dan Sperber or Pierre Lévy—the chief cybernetician of the French-speaking world, contributor to the review *Multitudes*, author of the aphorism: "Cosmic and cultural evolution culminates today in the virtual world of cyberspace."—to speak of "cybernetic communism." "Socialists and communists," Hardt and Negri write, "have long demanded that the proletariat have free access to and control over the machines and materials it uses to produce. In the context of immaterial and biopolitical production, however, this traditional demand takes on a new guise. The multitude not only uses machines to produce, but also becomes increasingly machinic itself, as the means of production are increasingly integrated into the minds and bodies of the multitude. In this context re-appropriation means having free access to and control over knowledge, information, communication, and affects—because these are some of the primary means of biopolitical production." In such a communism, they marvel, ONE will not share wealth but information and everyone will be both producer and consumer. Each of us will become our own "autonomedia"! Communism will be a communism of robots!

Whether it only breaks with the individualist postulates of the economy or it regards the commodity economy as a regional component of a more general economy—which is implied by all the discussions on the notion of value, like those of the German group, *Krisis*, all the Mauss-inspired defenses of the gift as against exchange, including the anti-cybernetic energetics of a Bataille, as well as all the reflections concerning the symbolic, whether on the part of Bourdieu or Baudrillard—the critique of political economy ultimately remains a tributary of economism. From the perspective of salvation through activity, the absence of a workers' movement corresponding to the revolutionary proletariat imagined by Marx will be compensated for by the militant work of its organization. "The party," writes Lyotard, "must furnish the proof that the proletariat is real and it can't do this any more than one can furnish the proof of a rational ideal. It can only furnish itself as proof and *practice a realistic politics*. The referent of its discourse remains unpresentable directly, nowhere to be seen. The repressed differend returns within the working-class movement, in particular in the form of recurrent conflicts around the question of organization." The quest for a class of producers engaged in struggle leads the most clearheaded Marxists to become *producers of an integrated class*. Now, it matters, existentially and strategically, whether we confront rather than produce social antagonisms, whether we are contradictors of the system and not among its regulators, whether we create, instead of hoping for a liberation of creativity, whether we desire rather than desiring desire, in short, whether we combat cybernetics instead of being *critical cyberneticians*.

Possessed by the sad passion of origins, one could look in historical socialism for the first indications of this alliance that has been obvious for thirty years, in Saint-Simon's philosophy of networks, for example, in Fourier's theory of equilibrium, or in Proudhon's mutualism, etc. But what socialists have had in common for two centuries, and what they share with those among them who declare themselves communists, is to struggle against a single effect of capitalism: in all its forms socialism struggles against separation by recreating social ties between subjects, between subjects and objects, without contesting the totalization by which THEY can assimilate the social to a body and the individual to a closed entity, a body-subject. But there is also another shared, mystical ground, on the basis of which the transfer of categories of thought between socialism and cybernetics has created an alliance, that of an unavowable humanism, an *unbridled* faith in the genius of humanity. Just as it's absurd to see "a collective soul" behind the construction of a hive starting from the erratic behavior of bees, as Maeterlinck did from a Catholic perspective at the beginning of the 20th century, the maintenance of capitalism is not in any way contingent on the existence of a collective consciousness of the "multitude" lodged at the center of production. By way of the axiom of class struggle, the historical socialist utopia, the utopia of *the* community, would ultimately be a utopia of the One imposed by the Head on a body that has no say in the matter. Today every socialism, by identifying more or less explicitly with the categories of democracy, production, and social contract, defends the party of cybernetics. Non-civil politics should understand itself as anti-social to the same degree that it is anti-State, it must refuse to contribute to the resolution of the "social question," take no part in the framing of the world in terms of problems, reject the democratic perspective that structures everybody's acceptance of *society's* demands. *As for cybernetics, today it's nothing more than the last possible socialism.*

VII

"Theory is the pleasure of immobilization [...] What gives you a hard-on, theoreticians, and throws you onto our [libidinal] band, is the chill of the clear and distinct; in fact, of the distinct alone, that is, the opposable, for the clear is only a suspect residue of the distinct, translated into a philosophy of the subject. Stop the [disjunctive] bar, you say: get out of this pathos—this is your pathos."
—Jean-François Lyotard, *Économie libidinal*, 1973

It is customary when one is a writer, poet, or philosopher to speak of the power of the Word to obstruct, confound, break through the informational flows of Empire, the binary machines of enunciation. You've heard the champions of poetry as the last rampart confronting the barbarism of communication. The author, even when they identify their position with that of the minor literatures, the eccentrics, the "literary madmen or women," when they search out the idiolects that shape every language to show that which escapes the code, to implode the very idea of comprehension, to expose the fundamental misunderstanding that causes the tyranny of information to fail, the author who, moreover, knows they are acted upon, spoken, traversed by intensities, remains motivated nonetheless, in front of their blank page, by a prophetic conception of the written word. For the "receiver" that I am, the disorientation effects that certain writing styles have deliberately sought, starting in the 1960s, are no less paralyzing than the old categorical and sententious critical theory. To see, from the chair where I sit, Guyotat or

Guattari getting off at every line, contorting, belching, farting, and vomiting their becoming-delirium doesn't arouse me, make me come, make me rant except rarely, that is, when a desire carries me to the shores of voyeurism. Performances for sure but performances of what? Performances of a boarding school alchemy in which the philosopher's stone is sought with spurts of ink and semen mixed together. The proclaimed *intensity* is not sufficient to engender the *passage* of intensity. Theory and criticism, for their part, remain cloistered in a policing of the clear and distinct statement, as transparent as the passage from "false consciousness" to enlightened consciousness was supposed to be.

Far from giving in to any sort of mythology of the Word or essentialism of meaning, Burroughs proposes in *Electronic Revolution* forms of struggle against the controlled circulation of statements, offensive strategies of enunciation that come out of the operations of "mental manipulation" inspired by his experiments with the "cut-up," an assemblage of statements based on chance. To be sure, in proposing to make "scrambling" into a revolutionary weapon, he's continuing the previous attempts to find an offensive language. But like the Situationist practice of *détournement*, which nothing in its *modus operandi* allows us to distinguish from that of "cooptation"—a fact that explains its spectacular success—"scrambling" is only a reactive operation. The same is true of the contemporary forms of struggle on the Internet that are inspired by these instructions by Burroughs: pirating, virus propagations, or overloading can ultimately only serve to temporarily destabilize the functioning of the communication network. But for what concerns us here and now, Burroughs is forced to admit, in terms inherited, it should be said, from the theories of communication, which reify the transmitter-receiver relation, that: "It would be more useful to discover how the models of exploration could be altered to enable the subject to free up their own spontaneous models." What matters with every verbal expression [*énonciation*] is not reception but contagion. I call *insinuation*—the *illiapsus* of medieval philosophy—the strategy that consists in following the sinuosity of thought, the errant words that reach me while also constituting the vacant lot where their reception will make a place for itself. By playing on the relationship between the sign and its referents, by repurposing clichés, such as for caricature, by letting the reader draw near, insinuation makes an encounter possible, an intimate presence, between the subject of the enunciation and those who make connections with the enunciated. "There are passwords beneath order-words," Deleuze and Guattari write, "words that pass, words that are components of a passage, whereas order-words mark stoppages or organized, stratified compositions." Insinuation is the haze of theory and is well suited to a discourse whose purpose is to enable struggles against the cult of transparency attached, from the origin, to the cybernetic hypothesis.

The fact that the cybernetic worldview is an abstract machine, a mystical fable, a cold eloquence from which multiple bodies, gestures, spoken expressions constantly escape, should not lead to the conclusion that it is bound to fail. If cybernetics lacks something in this respect, that is the very thing that sustains it: the enjoyment of outrageous rationalization, the burning sensation brought on by "tautologism," the passion for reduction, the pleasure of binary flattening. *Tackling the cybernetic hypothesis, it bears repeating, doesn't mean critiquing it and imposing a competing vision of the social world in its stead but experimenting in its vicinity, establishing other protocols, creating them from scratch and taking pleasure in that.* Beginning in the 1950s, the cybernetic hypothesis exerted an unacknowledged fascination on a whole "critical" generation, from the Situationists to Castoriadis, from Lyotard to Foucault, Deleuze, and Guattari. One could map their responses in this way: the former opposed it by developing a thought situated outside and above; the latter by using a thought from the middle; that is, on the one hand, "a metaphysical type of differend with the world that looks toward transcendent supra-terrestrial worlds or utopian counter-worlds," on the other, "a poietic type of differend with the world that sees in the real itself the path leading to freedom," as Peter Sloterdijk encapsulates it. The success of any future revolutionary experimentation will be measured essentially by its ability to make this contrast obsolete. That begins when bodies adopt a different scale, sense themselves thickening, are traversed by molecular phenomena that escape the systemic points of view, the molar representations, and make their every pore a vision machine attached to becomings rather than a camera that enframes, that delimits, that assigns beings. In the lines that follow, I insinuate a protocol of experimentation designed to undo the cybernetic hypothesis and the world it goes on constructing. But as with other erotic or strategic arts, its use is not something that's decided or imposed, it can only come from the purest involuntarism, which involves a certain casualness.

VIII

"*We lack that generosity, that indifference to fate which is given, in the absence of a great joy, by familiarity with the worst deprivations and which the coming world will bring to us.*"
— *Roger Caillois*

"*The fictitious constantly pays a higher price for its strength when beyond its screen the possible real becomes visible. It's only today, no doubt, that the domination of the fictitious has become totalitarian. But this is precisely its dialectical and 'natural' limit. Either in the final trial by fire, desire itself disappears and along with it its subject, the developing corporeity of the latent* Gemeinwesen, *or every simulacrum is cleared away: the extreme struggle of the species is unleashed against the managers of alienation and, in the bloody sinking of all the 'suns of the future,' there begins to dawn a possible future at last. Henceforth, in order to be, humans only need to separate themselves once and for all from every 'concrete utopia.'*"
— Giorgio Cesarano, *Manuel de survie*, 1975

All the individuals, groups, all the forms-of-life cannot be loaded into a feedback loop. Some of them are too fragile. They threaten to break. Or too strong, and they threaten to *break*.
Those particular becomings,
on the point of breaking,
assume that at a moment of lived experience bodies go through the intense feeling
that it could end abruptly,
from one moment to the next,
that the nothing,
that silence,
that death are within reach of the body and the act.
It can end.
The threat.

Disabling the process of cybernetization, toppling the Empire, will require an opening to *panic*. Because Empire is a set of apparatuses aimed at forestalling and precluding the event, a process of control and rationalization, its collapse will always be imagined by its agents and agencies of control as the most irrational of phenomena. The lines that follow give an idea of what such a cybernetic perspective on panic would be and indicate, *a contrario*, panic's effective potential. "Panic is therefore an *ineffectual* collective behavior because it doesn't correspond to the (real or supposed) danger. It is characterized by mental regression to an archaic or gregarious level; it culminates in primitive reactions of frantic escape, disorderly agitation, physical violence and, in a general way, acts of self- or hetero-destructiveness. Panic reactions are due to characteristics of the collective mind, with an alteration of perceptions and judgment, an alignment with the crudest behaviors, suggestibility, and participation in violence without any notion of individual responsibility."

Panic is what makes cyberneticians panic. It represents *absolute risk*, the permanent potential threat offered by the intensification of relations between forms-of-life. That being the case, it has to be made frightening as the same paid cybernetician tries to do: "Panic is dangerous for the population it strikes; it increases the number of victims resulting from an accident because of the inappropriate escape reactions, it can even be the only thing responsible for deaths and injuries: it's the same scenarios over and over again: acts of blind rage, trampling, crushing..." The deceit of such a description consists in imagining panic phenomena exclusively in a closed space: as a liberation of bodies, panic self-destroys because everyone attempts to escape through an exit that is too narrow.

But it is possible to envisage, like at Genoa in July 2001, that a panic on a large enough scale to disrupt the cybernetic controls and cross through several environments, goes beyond the stage of annihilation, as Canetti suggests in *Crowds and Power*: "If they were not in a theatre, people could flee together like a herd of animals in danger, and increase the impetus of their flight by the simultaneity of identical movements. An active crowd-fear of this kind is the common collective experience of all animals who live together in herds and whose joint safety depends on their speed." In this connection, I regard as a political fact of the greatest importance the panic of more than a million persons that Orson Welles provoked in October 1938 by announcing on the radio the imminent arrival of Martians in New Jersey, during a time when radio broadcasting was new enough for people to still attach a certain truth value to what it broadcast. Because "the more fiercely each man fights for his life, the clearer it becomes that he is fighting against all the others who hem him in," panic also reveals, together with an extraordinary and uncontrollable expenditure, civil war in its raw state: it is "a disintegration of the crowd *within* the crowd."

In a situation of panic, communities detach from the social body conceived as a totality and want to escape from it. But since they are still its captives physically and socially they are obliged to attack it. Panic manifests, more than any other phenomena, the plural and inorganic body of the species. Sloterdijk, that last man of philosophy, expands on this positive conception of panic: "From a historical perspective, the alternatives are probably the first men to develop a non-hysterical relation with the possible apocalypse [...] Current alternative consciousness is characterized by something one could label a pragmatic relationship with catastrophe." To the question, "Insofar as it must be built on hopes, repetitions, securities, and institutions, doesn't civilization depend on the absence, indeed the exclusion, of the panic element?," as the cybernetic hypothesis implies, Sloterdijk counters that "it is only thanks to the proximity of panic experiences that lively civilizations are possible." In this way they stave off the catastrophic potentialities of the epoch while rediscovering their native familiarity. They offer the possibility of *converting these energies* into "a *rational ecstasy* through which the individual opens him- or herself to the intuition: 'I am the world.'" Seeking active panic—"the panic experience of the world"—is therefore a technique of assumption of the risk of disintegration that each of us represents for society as a risky dividual. It's the end of hope and of every concrete utopia that takes form as a bridge extended towards the fact of no longer expecting anything, of having nothing left to lose. And through a particular sensitivity to the possibilities of lived situations, to their possibilities of collapse, to the extreme fragility of their sequencing, it's a way of reintroducing a serene relationship with the headlong rush of cybernetic capitalism. At the twilight of nihilism, it's a matter of making fear just as *extravagant* as hope.

In the framework of the cybernetic hypothesis, panic is understood as a change of state of the self-regulated system. For a cybernetician, every disorder can only start with variations between measured behaviors and effective behaviors of elements of the system. So-called "noise" is a behavior that would escape control while remaining refractory to the system, that is, one that cannot be processed by a binary machine, reduced to a 0 or a 1. Such noises are the lines of escape, the divagations of desires that are not yet entered into the circuit of valorization—the non-inscribed. We have called Imaginary Party the heterogeneous ensemble of these noises that proliferate *under* the Empire without however upsetting its unstable equilibrium, without altering its state, solitude for example being the most widespread form of these crossings over to the side of the Imaginary Party. When he founds the cybernetic hypothesis, Wiener imagines the existence of systems—called "reverberating closed circuits"—in which variances between the desired behaviors of the whole and the effective behaviors of the elements would proliferate. He envisages that these noises might increase dramatically in series, as when the reactions of a driver oversteer their vehicle when they've come upon an icy patch or scraped a highway guardrail. An overproduction of bad feedbacks that distort what they should signal, that amplify what they should contain—these situations indicate the path of a pure *reverberating force*. The current practice of bombarding certain nodal points of the Internet with information—"denial-of-service"—aims at producing such situations. All revolt under and against Empire can only be conceived on the basis of these "noises" capable of constituting what Prigogine and Stengers—who suggest an analogy between the physical world and the social world—have called "bifurcation points," critical thresholds by means of which a new state of the system becomes possible.

The shared mistake of Marx and Bataille with their categories of "labor capacity" or "expenditure" was to have located the potential for overthrowing the system *outside the circulation of commodity flows*, in a pre-systemic exteriority, prior to or after capitalism, in nature (Marx) or in a foundational sacrifice (Bataille), that would be the lever from which to analyze the endless metamorphoses of the capitalist system. In the first issue of *Le Grand Jeu*, the problem of equilibrium breakdown is formulated in more immanent if somewhat ambiguous terms: "This force that exists cannot remain unemployed in a cosmos that is as full as an egg and within which everything acts and reacts on everything. Except that then there is a sudden shift, an unknown lever will make this current of violence swerve in another direction. Or rather in a parallel direction, but thanks to the sudden shift, on a different plane. Its revolt will become the invisible Revolt." It's not a matter simply of an "invisible insurrection of a million minds" as the celestial Trocchi thought. The force that we call *ecstatic politics* does not come from a substantial outside but from the deviation, the small variation, the gyrations that, starting from the system's interior, push it locally to its breaking point and hence the intensities that pass once again between forms-of-life, despite the reduced level of intensities they maintain. More exactly, it comes from the desire that exceeds the flow insofar as it feeds the latter without being traceable there, that it passes *beneath its trace*, sometimes settling there, instantiating itself between forms-of-life that, in a situation, play the role of attractors. As we know, it is in the nature of desire not to leave traces where it passes. Let's return to that moment when a system in equilibrium can totter. "When we come close to the bifurcation points," write Prigogine and Stengers, "there where the system has the 'choice' between two regimes of functioning and is not, strictly speaking, in the one or in the other, the deviation from the general law is total: the fluctuations can attain the same order of magnitude as the average macroscopic values. [...] Regions separated by macroscopic distances are correlated: the speeds of the reactions produced there adjust to one another, so the local events reverberate through the whole system. It's truly a matter of a paradoxical state that defies all our "intuitions" about the behavior of populations, a state in which small differences, far from cancelling each other out, succeed each other and spread without stopping. In this way, the indifferent chaos of equilibrium has given way to a *fertile chaos* from which different structures can emerge."

It would be naïve to deduce a new political art directly from this scientific description of the potentials for disorder. The error of philosophers and of any thought that unfolds without recognizing, in its very enunciation, what it owes to desire, is to place oneself artificially above the processes it objectifies, even in the experimental context—a shortcoming, moreover, that Prigogine and Stengers don't manage to avoid. Experimentation, which is not the completed experiment but its process of accomplishment, is situated *in* the fluctuation, *in the midst of the noises,* on the lookout for the bifurcation. Events that are verified in the social, at a level meaningful enough to influence general destinies, do not form a simple summation of individual behaviors. Nor do individual behaviors by themselves influence general destinies. There remain nonetheless three stages that go together as one and that, without being represented, will be experienced by bodies as immediately political problems: I have in mind the amplification of non-conforming acts; the intensification of desires and their rhythmic harmony; and the organization of a territory, given that "the fluctuation that leads from one regime to the other cannot possibly over-run the initial state in a single move. It must first establish itself in a region. Depending on whether the size of the initial fluctuation lies below or above some critical value [...] the fluctuation regresses or else spreads through the whole system." Three problems therefore that call for exercises in prepara-tion for an anti-imperial offensive: *the problem of force, the problem of rhythm, the problem of momentum.*

These questions, considered from the neutralized or neutralizing viewpoint of the laboratory or armchair observer, must be taken up and tested out by oneself. What does amplifying fluctuations mean to me? How can deviances, mine for example, provoke disorder? How does one go from scattered and singular fluctuations, from each one's divergences from the norm and the apparatuses, to becomings, to destinies? How can what flees in capitalism, what escapes valorization, gather force and turn back against capitalism? Classic politics solved this problem by mobilization. Mobilizing meant adding, aggregating, assembling, synthesizing. It meant unifying the small differences that the fluctuations make, depicting them as a great wrong, an irreparable injustice, to be righted. The singularities were already there. It sufficed to subsume them under a single predicate. The energy too was already there. It sufficed to organize it. I will be the head, they will be the body. Thus the theoretician, the vanguard, the party made force function in the same way as capitalism, by means of putting into circulation and under control with the goal of seizing, as in classic warfare, the enemy's heart and taking power by taking its head.

The invisible revolt, the "world coup" that Trocchi spoke of, relies instead on potential [*puissance*]. It is invisible because it is unforeseeable in the eyes of the imperial system. Amplified, fluctuations as opposed to the imperial apparatuses never aggregate.

They are as *heterogeneous* as desires are and will never be able to form any closed totality, not even a multitude whose name is only a ploy if it doesn't designate the *irreconcilable multiplicity* of forms-of-life. Desires flee, they trace a clinamen or not, they produce intensities or not, and beyond their flight they continue to flee. They remain resistant to every form of representation as a body, a class, a party. So one has to deduce that every propagation of fluctuations will also be a propagation of civil war. The diffuse *guerilla* is the only form of warfare that will produce this kind of invisibility in the eyes of the enemy. The recourse to diffuse guerilla warfare by a fraction of Autonomia in the Italy of the 1970s is explainable precisely by reference to the advanced cybernetic character of Italian governmentality. Those were the years that saw the development of "consociationalism," which heralded the present-day "citizenism," the joining together of parties, unions, and associations to allocate and co-manage power. Again the most important thing here is not the sharing but the management and the control. This mode of government goes well beyond the welfare State in creating longer chains of interdependence between citizens and apparatuses, extending in this way the principles of control and management of the administrative bureaucracy.

IX

"It's here that generalized programs are stymied. They can't handle bits of the world, pieces of men that want nothing to do with them, with generalized programs."
— Philippe Carles, Jean-Louis Comolli, "Free Jazz, hors programme, hors sujet, hors champ," 2000

"The few active rebels must have the qualities of speed and endurance, ubiquity and independence of arteries of supply."
— *T.E. Lawrence,* "Guerilla Warfare," *Encyclopaedia Britannica*, volume X, 1926

We have T.E. Lawrence to thank for having elaborated the principles of guerilla warfare on the basis of his combat experience with the Arabs against the Turks in 1916. What does Lawrence say? That battle is no longer the only process of war, just as destruction of the enemy core is no longer its central objective, *a fortiori* if that enemy is faceless as is the case when one faces the impersonal power materialized by the cybernetic apparatuses of Empire: "Most wars are wars of contact, both forces striving to keep in contact to avoid tactical surprise. The Arab war should be a war of detachment: to contain the enemy by the silent threat of a vast unknown desert, not disclosing themselves till the moment of attack." Deleuze, though he posits too rigid a contrast between the *guerilla*, which raises the problem of individuality, and war, which raises that of collective organization, specifies that it's a matter of clearing as much space as possible and envisioning, or better still, "fashioning some reality and no longer responding to what is given as real." The invisible revolt and the diffuse *guerilla* don't punish an injustice, they create a possible world. In the language of the cybernetic hypothesis, at the molecular level I am able to create the invisible revolt, or the diffuse *guerilla* in two ways. First gesture, I fashion some reality, I disrupt and I disrupt myself in the same act. All sabotage has its source there. What my behavior represents at that moment does not exist for the apparatus that is sabotaged along with me. Neither 0 nor 1, I am the absolute third. My pleasure exceeds the capacity of the apparatus. Second gesture, I don't respond to the human or machine feedback loops that attempt to encircle me, like Bartleby I "prefer not to," I stand apart, I don't connect, I stay put. I use my passivity as a force against the apparatuses. Neither 0 nor 1, I am the absolute nothingness. First phase: I take my pleasure perversely. Second phase: I reserve myself. Beyond. Elsewhere. *Short circuit and disconnection.* In both cases the feedback doesn't take place, there is the beginning of a line of flight. An external line of flight on the one hand, that seems to issue from me; an internal line of flight on the other hand that brings me back to myself. All forms of jamming are based on these two gestures, external and internal lines of flight, sabotages and withdrawals, the search for forms of struggle and the assumption of forms-of-life. Henceforth the revolutionary problem will consist in combining these two moments.

Lawrence relates that this was also the question that had to be resolved by the Arabs with whom he aligned himself against the Turks. Their tactics in fact "were always tip and run; not pushes, but strokes. The Arab army never tried to maintain or improve an advantage, but to move on and strike again somewhere else. It used the smallest force in the quickest time at the farthest place." Attacks against materiel and especially against the channels of communication, such as depriving a section of railroad of its rails, were privileged over those against the institutions themselves. The rebellion becomes invisible only to the extent that it attains its objective, which is to "deny the adversary any objective," to never offer targets to the enemy. In this case it imposed on the enemy a "passive defense" that was very costly in men and materials, *in energies*, and that stretched the enemy's front while linking together its own points of attack. Hence guerilla warfare tended from its invention toward the diffuse *guerilla*. This type of combat produces, moreover, new relations that are quite distinct from those that obtain in traditional armies: "Maximum irregularity and articulation were the aims. Diversity threw the enemy intelligence off the track… Any of the Arabs could go home whenever the conviction failed him. The only contract was honor. Consequently the Arab army had no discipline, in the strict sense in which it is restrictive, submergent of individuality, the lowest common denominator of men." Yet Lawrence doesn't idealize the libertarian spirit of his troops, as spontaneists in general are prone to do. The crucial thing is to be able to count on a sympathizing population which then serves as a place of potential recruitment and of propagation of the struggle. "Rebellions can be made by 2% in a striking force and 98% passively sympathetic," but this requires time and propaganda operations. At the same time, all the offensives aimed at confusing the enemy lines will depend on a perfect intelligence service "so that plans can be made in complete certainty" and the enemy will never be provided with an objective. This function of intelligence and transmission of accumulated powers/ knowledges is precisely the role that an organization, in the sense the term had in classic politics, could have henceforth. Thus the spontaneity of *guerilleros* does not necessarily rule out some kind of organization as a reservoir of strategic information.

But the important thing is that the practice of jamming, as Burroughs conceives it, and the hackers after him, is futile if it is not accompanied by an organized practice of intelligence about domination. This necessity is strengthened by the fact that the space in which the invisible revolt could take place is not the desert that Lawrence talks about.

Nor is the electronic space of the Internet the smooth and neutral space spoken of by the ideologues of the information age. The most recent studies confirm moreover that the Internet is at the mercy of a targeted and coordinated attack. The interconnection was designed in such a way that the network would still function after a loss of 99% of the ten million routers—the network communication nodes where information is concentrated—destroyed in a random way, in line with what the American military had initially wanted. However, a selective attack based on precise intelligence about the traffic, and targeting 5% of the most strategic nodes—the nodes of the high-speed networks of the major operators, the entry points of the transatlantic cables—would be enough to provoke a collapse of the system. Virtual or real, the spaces of Empire are structured into territories, striated by cascades of devices that trace the boundaries then erase them when they become useless, in a constant sweep that is the very motor of circulation flows. And in such a structured, territorialized, and deterritorialized space, the front line with the enemy cannot be as clear-cut as in Lawrence's desert. Consequently, the floating character of power, the nomadic dimension of domination require an increased amount of intelligence activity, which means an organization of the circulation of knowledges/powers. This should be the role of the Society for the Advancement of Criminal Science (SACS).

In *Cybernetics and Society*, at a time when he sensed belatedly that the political use of cybernetics tended to reinforce the exercise of domination, Wiener asked himself a similar question, preliminary to the mystical crisis in which he would finish his life: "The whole technique of secrecy, message jamming, and bluff is concerned with insuring that one's own side can make use of the forces and agencies of communication more effectively than the other side. In this combative use of information *it is quite as important to keep one's own message channels open as to obstruct the other side in the use of the channels available to it*. An over-all policy in matters of secrecy almost always must involve the consideration of many more things than secrecy itself." The problem of force reformulated into a problem of invisibility becomes therefore *a problem of modulation of opening and closing*. It demands both organization and spontaneity. Or to say it differently, the diffuse *guerilla* requires constituting *two distinct planes of consistency*, distinct but interleaved, a first where the opening is organized, where the interplay of forms-of-life is transformed into information, a second where the closing is organized, that is, the resistance of the forms-of-life to their informatization. Curcio: "The guerilla party is the maximal agent of invisibility and externalization with respect to the enemy cohabiting in it at the highest level of synthesis." It will be objected that, after all, this is just another form of binary machine, neither better nor less good than those operating in cybernetics. This will be wrong, because it's not to see that at the basis of these two gestures there is a fundamental distance with respect to the regulated flows, a distance that is the very prerequisite for experience in a world of apparatuses, a distance that is a potential [*puissance*] which I can convert into a thickness and into a becoming. But it will be wrong above all because it fails to understand that the alternation between sovereignty and powerlessness [*impouvoir*] is not programmable, that the trajectory these two postures project is an errant one, that the places that end up getting selected, on the body, at the factory, in the urban and near-urban non-places, are unpredictable.

X

"Revolution is movement, but movement is not revolution."
—Paul Virilio, *Vitesse et politique*, 1977

In a world of well-ordered storylines, minutely calculated programs, impeccable scores, well-placed options and actions, what obstructs, what shuffles, what limps?
Limping indicates the body.
The corporal.
Limping indicates man of the fragile heel.
A God held him by that. He was God by virtue of the heel. The Gods hobble, when they aren't hunchbacked.
Malfunction is the body. That which limps, hurts, is unsteady, barely stands, out of breath and the miracle of balance. Music doesn't stand upright any more than man does.
Bodies are not yet well-ordered by the law of the commodity. The things don't function. They suffer. They tire out. They make mistakes. They walk off.
Too hot, too cold, too near, too far, too fast, too slow.
— Philippe Carles, Jean-Louis Comolli, "Free Jazz, hors programme, hors sujet, hors champ," 2000

People have often emphasized—T.E. Lawrence is not an exception—the kinetic dimension of politics and war as a strategic counterpoint to a quantitative conception of force relations. This is typically the perspective of guerilla warfare as against that of traditional warfare. It has been said that, unless it's massive, a movement needs to be swift, more rapid than the prevailing domination. For example, this is how the Situationist International formulated its program in 1957: "It should be understood that we are going to assist, participate in, a speed race between free artists to experiment with and develop the new techniques of conditioning. In this race the police already have a sizable advantage. On its outcome, however, depends the emergence of exciting and emancipatory environments or the strengthening—scientifically controllable, without gaps—of the old-world environment of oppression and horror. [...] If control of these new means is not totally revolutionary, we can be led toward the civilized ideal of a colony of bees." Faced with this last image, an explicit but *static* evocation of fully-developed cybernetics in the guise of Empire, revolution should consist in a re-appropriation of the most modern technological tools, a re-appropriation that should make it possible to challenge policing on its own terrain, by creating a counter-world with the same means as those it employs. Here speed is thought of as one of the important qualities for the revolutionary political art. But this strategy is predicated on attacking sedentary forces. The thing is that under Empire the latter tend to crumble whereas the impersonal power of the apparatuses becomes nomadic and permeates all the institutions while causing them to implode.

To the contrary, it is slowness that has informed another part of the struggle against Capital. Luddist sabotage should not be interpreted from a traditional Marxist perspective as nothing more than a primitive rebellion compared to what the organized proletariat does, as a protest by reactionary craft workers against the gradual expropriation of the means of production caused by industrialization. It is, rather, a deliberate act of *slowing down* the flows of commodities and persons, which is done in anticipation of the central characteristic of cybernetic capitalism insofar as it is movement towards movement, will to power, generalized acceleration. Moreover, Taylor conceived of the "scientific management" of labor as a technique for combating "worker slowdown" that represented a real obstacle to production. In the physical order, mutations of the system also depend on a certain slowness, as Prigogine and Stengers point out: "The faster communication takes place within a system, the greater the percentage of unsuccessful fluctuations and thus the more stable the system." Slowdown tactics carry an additional force, therefore, in the struggle against cybernetic capitalism because they attack it not just in its being but in its process as well. But that is not all: slowness is necessary for bringing forms-of-life into a mutual relation that is not reducible to a mere exchange of information. It expresses the relation's resistance to interaction.

Beneath or beyond the speed and slowness of communication, there is the space of *encounter* that marks an absolute limit to the analogy between the social world and the physical world. Indeed it's because two particles *will never encounter each other* that rupture phenomena cannot be deduced from laboratory observations. The encounter is that abiding instant when intensities manifest between forms-of-life that are *present* in everyone. Beneath the social and communication, it is the territory that actualizes the potentialities of bodies and actualizes itself in the differences of intensity that they release, that they are. The encounter is situated

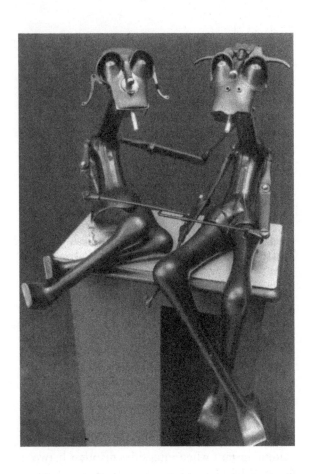

beneath language, beyond words, in the unsettled land of the unsaid, at the level of a deferral, of that potentiality of the world which is also its negation, its "power-not-to-be." What is the other? "Another *possible* world," answers Deleuze. The other embodies this possibility the world has of not being, or of being other. This is why in so-called "primitive" societies war assumes that primordial importance of annihilating any other possible world. It is pointless, however, to consider conflict without considering pleasure [*jouissance*], war without considering love. Every tumultuous awakening to love awakens the fundamental desire to transform oneself while transforming the world. The aversion and suspicion that lovers arouse around them are the automatic and defensive response to the war they wage, just from the fact of loving each other, against a world in which every passion will go unacknowledged and fade away.

With the encounter, violence is thus the first rule of the game. Violence is what polarizes the vagaries of desire, whose sovereign liberty Lyotard invokes in his *Économie libidinale*. But because he refuses to see that the pleasures [*jouissances*] are harmonious amongst themselves on a terrain that precedes them and where the forms-of-life rub shoulders with each other, because he refuses to understand that the neutralization of every intensity is itself an intensification, nothing like the neutralization of Empire, and because he can't deduce that everything being inseparable, life drives and death drives aren't neutral in the face of a singular other, in the end Lyotard can't go beyond the hedonism that is most compatible with cybernetization: let yourself go, live it up, give free rein to your desires! Take your pleasure [*Jouissez*], enjoy, there will always be something left! There is no doubt that conduction, abandon, mobility in general can help amplify deviation from the norm, provided one recognizes that which, in the very midst of circulation, breaks the flows. Confronting the acceleration that cybernetics provokes, speed and nomadism can only represent secondary elaborations in relation to *slow-down politics*.

Speed gives impetus to institutions. Slowness shuts off the flows. The strictly kinetic problem of politics is therefore not to choose between two types of revolt but to abandon oneself to a *pulsation*, to explore other intensifications than those prescribed by the temporality of urgency. The power of the cyberneticians has resided in giving a rhythm to the social body that tends to hinder any respiration. But rhythm is associated precisely with foot motion, at least as Canetti conceives it, in terms of its anthropological genesis: "Rhythm is originally the rhythm of the feet. Every human being walks, and, since he walks on two legs with which he strikes the ground in turn and since he only moves if he continues to do this, whether intentionally or not, a rhythmic sound ensues." And this foot motion is not predictable as would be that of a robot: "The two feet never strike the ground with exactly the same force. The difference between them can be larger or smaller according to individual constitution or mood. It is also possible to walk faster or slower, to run, to stand still suddenly, or to jump." This means that rhythm is the opposite of a program, that it depends on forms-of-life, and that problems of speed can be brought back to questions of rhythm. Being *precariously balanced*, every body carries with it a rhythm showing that it is in its nature to hold untenable positions. In light of this rhythm that comes from the lurchings of bodies, from the motions of the feet, Canetti adds that it is at the origin of writing in the form of tracks left by the movement of animals, that is, by History. The event is nothing other than the manifestation of such tracks and to make History is therefore to improvise in search of a rhythm. Whatever credence one gives to Canetti's demonstrations, they indicate, in the manner of true fictions, that political kinetics will be better understood as *a politics of rhythm*. This means *at a minimum* that the binary and techno rhythm imposed by cybernetics must be opposed by *different rhythms*.

But it also means that those other rhythms, as manifestations of an ontological imbalance, have always had a creative political function. Canetti, again, says that on the one hand, "steps added to steps in quick succession conjure up a larger number of men than there are. The men do not move away but, dancing, remain on the same spot. The sound of their steps does not die away, for these are continually repeated; there is a long stretch of time during which they continue to sound loud and *alive. What they lack in numbers they make up in intensity.*" On the other hand, "if they stamp harder, it sounds as if there were more of them. As long as they go on dancing, they exert an attraction on all in their neighborhood." Hence searching for the right rhythm creates an opening for the experience to intensify and for the numbers to increase. It's a means of aggregation as well as an action to be imitated. On the scale of the individual and that of society, bodies themselves lose their feeling of unity and multiply as potential weapons: "The equivalence of the participants becomes, and ramifies as, the equivalence of their limbs. Every part of a man which can move gains a life of its own and acts as if independent." So the politics of rhythm is also the search for a reverberation, for a *different state* comparable to a trance of the social body, through the ramification of every body. For there are in fact two possible regimes of rhythm in the cybernitized

Empire. The first, which Simondon refers to, is that of the technical man "who ensures the function of integration and extends the ongoing self-regulation to every monad of automation," technicians whose "life is made of the rhythm of the machines that surround him and that he connects to each other." The second rhythm aims at undermining this interconnection: it is deeply disintegrative without being simply spasmodic [*bruitiste*]. It is a *rhythm of disconnection*. The collective conquest of this *correct dissonant tempo* will have to involve a prior surrender to *improvisation*.

"Raising the curtain of words, improvisation becomes gesture,
act not yet said.
Form not yet named, normed, honored.
Abandon oneself to improvisation
To free oneself already from the world's narratives, lovely though they may be.
Already there, already lovely, already told, already world.
Undo, o Penelope, the musical ribbons that form our sound cocoon
which is not the world but the ritual habit of the world.

Abandoned, she offers herself to what floats around meaning,

around words,
around codifications,
she offers herself to intensities,
notes withheld, surges, energies,
that is, to what has no proper name.
[...]
Improvisation welcomes threat and passes beyond it, divests it of itself, makes note of it, potentiality and risk."

XI

"What comes to occupy this space is haze, solar haze. The rebellion itself is a gas, a vapor. Haze is the first state of nascent perception; it creates mirages in which things rise and fall, as if under the action of a piston, and men levitate, as if suspended from a rope. To see through a haze is to have blurred vision—the rough outlines of a hallucinatory perception, a cosmic gray. Does the gray then divide in two, producing black when the shadow appears or the light disappears, but also white when the luminous itself becomes opaque."
— Gilles Deleuze, "La honte et la gloire: T.E. Lawrence," *Critique et Clinique*, 1993

"Nothing and no one gives the gift of an alternative adventure: there's no other possible adventure than that of conquering a destiny for oneself. You can only complete this conquest by starting from the spatiotemporal site where 'your' things stamp you as being a thing of theirs."
— Giorgio Cesarano, *Manuel de Survie*, 1975

From the cybernetic perspective, threat cannot be welcomed and certainly not surpassed. It has to be absorbed, eliminated. I've already said that the endlessly renewed impossibility of that nullification of the event is the last certainty on which to base practices of opposition to the world governed by apparatuses. Threat, and its generalization in the form of panic, poses unresolvable energy problems for the defenders of the cybernetic hypothesis. In this connection, Simondon explains that machines that have a high information output, that control their environment precisely, have a low energy output. Conversely, machines that take little energy to carry out their cybernetic mission produce a poor yield of reality. The transformation of forms into information contains two contrary imperatives in fact: "Information is, in a sense, what brings a series of new, unpredictable states that don't belong to any pre-definable sequence. So it is what demands of the channel of information *an absolute availability* in regard to every aspect of the modulation it conveys; *the information channel must not itself contribute any predetermined form, must not be selective* [...] In a contrary sense, information is distinguishable from noise only because one can assign a certain code, a relative uniformization, to information; in cases where the noise cannot be directly reduced below a certain level, one brings about a *reduction of the margin of indetermination and unpredictability* of the signals." In other words, for a physical, biological, or social system to have enough energy to ensure its reproduction, it's necessary for the control apparatuses to cut into the bulk of the unknown, deciding between what falls under *pure randomness* and thus outside the control function, and what can enter into the latter as *contingency*, as something subject to an estimation of probability. It follows that for every apparatus, as in the specific case of sound recording devices, "a compromise must be adopted that preserves a sufficient yield of information for practical needs and an energy yield high enough to maintain the background noise at a level that doesn't disturb the signal level." In the case of the police for example this will involve finding the point of balance between repression—which has the function of diminishing the social background noise—and intelligence—which supplies information about the state and movements of the social complex on the basis of the signals it emits.

Hence provoking panic will mean first of all *expanding the background haze* that is superimposed on the triggering of feedback loops, which makes it costly for the cybernetic equipment to track behavioral deviances. Strategic thinking grasped the offensive significance of this haze early on. When Clausewitz notes for example that "popular resistance is obviously not capable of striking heavy blows" but that "like *something vaporous and fluid*, it must not condense anywhere." Lawrence contrasts traditional armies that "are like immobile plants," with the *guerilla*, comparable to "an influence, a thing invulnerable, intangible, without front or back, drifting about like a *gas*." *Haze is the privileged vector of revolt.* Transplanted into the cybernetic world, the metaphor also alludes to resistance to the tyranny of transparency that control imposes. In a short story titled "Love is blind," Boris Vian imagines what the effects of a very real fog would be on existing relationships. The inhabitants of a metropolis wake up one morning invaded by an "opaque tidal wave" that gradually alters all the behaviors. Things done for the sake of appearance are soon dropped and the city gives itself over to experimentation. The loves become free, facilitated by the constant nudity of all the bodies. Orgies spread. The skin, the hands, the flesh reclaim their prerogatives for "the realm of possibility expands when one is no longer afraid the lights will switch on." Unable to prolong a fog they didn't help to form, the inhabitants are distraught when "the radio announces that meteorologists are reporting a steady weakening of the phenomenon." As a result, all concerned decide to put out their eyes so that life will continue to be joyous. An assumption of destiny: the fog that Vian speaks of is conquered. It is conquered through a re-appropriation of violence, a re-appropriation that can go as far as mutilation. That kind of violence doesn't mean to teach anything, doesn't mean to construct anything, is not the political terror that good souls disparage. That violence consists entirely in the clearing away of defenses, in the opening of paths, of senses, of minds. "Is it ever pure?" asks Lyotard. "Is a *dance* true? One will always be able to say so. But that's not where its force [*puissance*] lies." To say that revolt must become haze means that it must become both dissemination and dissimulation. Just as the offensive must make itself opaque if it is to succeed, opacity must become offensive if it is to last. This is the index of the invisible revolt.

But this also indicates that its first objective will be to resist any attempt at reduction in the interest of representation. Haze is a vital response to the imperative of clarity, of transparency, which is the first stamp of imperial power on bodies. Becoming haze means that I finally take on the dark side that commands me to believe, and prevents me from believing, in all the fictions of direct democracy insofar as they would ritualize the transparency of each person to their own interest and of all to the interests of all. Becoming opaque like fog is to recognize that one doesn't represent anything, that one is not identifiable. It's to assume the unto-talizable character of the physical body and the political body as well. It's to open oneself to possibilities that are not yet known. It's to resist every struggle for recognition with all one's strength. Lyotard: "What you demand of us, theoreticians, is that we constitute ourselves as identities, and responsible ones at that! But if we are sure of anything, it is that this operation (of exclusion) is a sham, that incandescences are not the doing of anyone and they belong to no one." It should be said, however, that it won't be a matter of reconstituting some secret societies or belligerent conspiracies as was the case in Freemasonry, Carbonarism, and as the avant-gardes of the last century fantasized— I'm thinking in particular of the Collège de Sociologie. *Constituting a zone of opacity* in which to circulate and experiment freely without conducting the Empire's information flows is to produce "anonymous singularities," to recreate the conditions for a possible experiment, an experiment that is not immediately squashed by a binary machine that assigns it a meaning, a dense experiment that transforms desires and their instantiation into something beyond desires, into a narrative, into a thickened body. Thus when Toni Negri questions Deleuze about communism, the latter is careful not to assimilate it to a realized and transparent communication: "You ask whether control societies, communication societies, will lead to forms of resistance that might reopen the way for a communism understood as the 'transversal organization of free individuals.' Maybe, I don't know. But it would be nothing to do with minorities speaking out. Maybe speech and communication have been corrupted. They're thoroughly infiltrated by money—and not by accident but by their very nature. We've got to highjack [*détourner*] speech. Creating has always been something different from communicating. The key thing may be to create vacuoles of non-communication, circuit breakers, so we can elude control." Yes. The key thing for us is these zones of opacity, a creation of holes, of empty intervals, of *black blocs* in the cybernetic networks of power. Irregular war with Empire, on the scale of a place, a struggle, a riot, should begin with the construction of opaque and offensive zones. Each of these zones will be at the same time a *nucleus* on the basis of which to experiment and a *cloud* that spreads panic in the whole imperial system, a machine of coordinated warfare *and*

spontaneous subversion at every level. The proliferation of these zones of offensive opacity
(ZOO) and the intensification of their relations
will bring about an *irreversible* disequilibrium.

In order to indicate the conditions under which
opacity can be created, as a weapon and as a breaker
of flows, we should turn one last time to the internal critique of the cybernetic paradigm. Causing a
change of state in a physical or social system
requires that disorder, deviations from the norm,
be concentrated in a space, whether real or virtual.
In fact, for behavior fluctuations to spread like a
contagion they must first reach a "critical size," the
nature of which is explained by Prigogine and
Stengers: "It results from the fact that the 'outside
world,' the environment of the fluctuating region,
always tends to dampen fluctuations. Critical size
is a measure of the relationship between the volume,
where the reactions take place, and the surface of
contact, the interaction site. The critical size is thus
determined by the competition between the system's
'integrative power' and the chemical mechanisms
amplifying the fluctuation within the fluctuating
sub-region." This means that every deployment of
fluctuations in a system is bound to fail if it doesn't
have a prior local anchorage, a place from which
the deviations that reveal themselves might be
able to contaminate the whole system. Lawrence

confirms, once again: "Rebellion must have an *unassailable base*, something guarded not merely from attack, but from the fear of it." For such a place to exist it must have "independence of arteries of supply," without which no war is conceivable. If the question of bases is central in every revolt, this is also owing to the very principles of the balancing of systems. For cybernetics, the possibility of a contagion that overturns the system must be neutralized by the most immediate environment of the zone of autonomy where the fluctuations occur. This means that the effects of control are more powerful in the periphery nearest to the zone of offensive opacity that is created, around the fluctuating region. Consequently, the size of the base will have to be all the larger as the control is increased.

These bases must be as firmly inscribed in space as they are in minds. "The Arab revolt," explains Lawrence, "had such a base in the Red Sea ports, the desert, and in the minds of men converted to its creed." They are territories as much as they are mentalities. Let us call them *planes of consistency*. For the zones of offensive opacity to be formed and reinforced, it's necessary that such planes exist, that they link the deviations [*écarts*] together, that they serve as a lever, as a ground for the overcoming of fear. Historical Autonomy, possible Autonomy—

that of Italy in the 1970s for example—is nothing other than the persistence of active planes of consistency that form themselves into *unrepresentable spaces*, into bases of secession from society. The cyberneticians' critical re-appropriation of the category of autonomy—along with its derived notions of self-organization, autopoiesis, self-reference, self-valorization, etc.—is, from this viewpoint, the central maneuver of the past twenty years. Through the cybernetic prism, adopting one's own laws and producing subjectivities doesn't in any way contradict the production of the system and its regulation. By calling ten years ago for a multiplication of Temporary Autonomous Zones (TAZ) in both the real world and the virtual world, Hakim Bey thus remained a victim of the idealism of those who wish to abolish politics without first thinking it through. He found himself forced to separate, within the TAZ, the locus of hedonistic practices, of the "libertarian" expression of forms-of-life, from the locus of political resistance, from the form of struggle. If autonomy is considered here as being temporary, this is because to think of it as something *lasting* would require conceiving of a struggle coordinated with living, envisaging for example the *transmission of warrior skills*. Bey's type of liberals-libertarians are oblivious of the field of intensities where their sovereignty demands to deploy itself, and their idea of a social contract without a State basically supposes an identity of all beings since it's ultimately a matter of maximizing one's pleasures in peace, till the end of time. On the one hand, the TAZ are defined as "free enclaves," places whose law is liberty, fine things, the Marvelous. On the other, secession from the world they issue from, the "folds" in which they lodge themselves between the real and its coding would be constituted only after a series of "refusals." By positing autonomy as an attribute of individual or collective subjects, this "California ideology" deliberately conflates two incommensurable planes, the "self-realization" of persons and the "self-organization" of the social. This is because in the history of philosophy autonomy is an ambiguous notion that expresses both emancipation from every constraint *and* submission to higher natural laws, so that it can even be used to feed the hybrid, reframing discourses of the "anarcho-capitalist" cyborgs.

The autonomy that I speak of, however, is not temporary or merely defensive. It is not a substantial quality of beings but the essential condition of their becoming. It doesn't start from the hypothetical unity of the Subject but gives rise to multiplicities. It doesn't just attack the sedentary forms of power, such as the State, and then go surfing on its circulating, "mobile," "flexible" forms. It equips itself with the means to last as well as to move about, to withdraw as well as attack, to open out and close off, to link silent bodies as well as bodiless voices. It thinks of this alternation as being the result of an endless experimentation. "Autonomy" means that we cause the worlds that we are to grow. Empire, armed with cybernetics, demands autonomy for itself alone as a unitary system of the totality: it is thus constrained to destroy every autonomy insofar as it is heterogeneous. We say that autonomy is everyone's to claim and that the struggle for autonomy must intensify. The current form the civil war is taking is first of all that of a combat against the monopoly on autonomy. This experimentation spells "fertile chaos," communism, the end

of the cybernetic hypothesis.